The Easter Book

FRANCIS X. WEISER

The Easter Book

ILLUSTRATED BY ROBERT FRANKENBERG

St. Augustine Academy Press
Homer Glen, Illinois

This edition reprinted in 2018
by St. Augustine Academy Press

ISBN: 978-1-64051-055-5

Proceeds from the sale of this book will be donated to a fund for the support of Seminarians studying for the priesthood.

IMPRIMI POTEST: William E. FitzGerald, S.J., Provincial
NIHIL OBSTAT: Francis S. Rossiter, D.D., Diocesan Censor
IMPRIMATUR: ✠ Richard J. Cushing, D.D., Archbishop of Boston
DATE: October 29, 1953

ACKNOWLEDGMENTS: To Mrs. Foster Stearns, Editor of the *Herbarist*, Exeter, N.H., and to Daniel J. Foley, Boston, Mass., for permission to use material on Mary gardens. To Polanie Publishing Co., Minneapolis, Minn., for permission to reprint some recipes. To Marymount Publications, Cleveland, O., for permission to reprint the music of a Polish hymn. To the Chinese Sisters of the Franciscan Missionaries of Mary, for permission to print the music of a Chinese hymn. To Edward C. Currie for his assistance in research on music, and to Rev. Claude Klarkowski for providing and translating Polish texts. Also to Rev. Hugo Rahner, S.J., Rev. William A. Donaghy, S.J., Lajos I. Szathmáry, Lars Lund, Mrs. Mary Stack McNiff, Kevin Doherty, S.J., and members of Weston College Choir.

The notes referred to by number throughout the text are to be found at the end of the book.

Figures in parentheses after the names of persons indicate the year of death.

Foreword

The feast of Easter marks the climax of liturgy and, with Christmas, the most celebrated of Christian seasons and holydays. Easter Sunday is a dazzling diamond that radiates the splendor of Redemption and Resurrection into the hearts of the faithful everywhere. Its various facets cast the brilliance of eternity over the twilight of time, and enrapture the soul with the deathless pledge of a Second Spring. The keener are the eyes of faith, the more penetrating is the vision of personal immortality behind the veil of death: When Christ rose, Death itself died.

As in *The Christmas Book*, I have tried also in this book on Easter and the Easter season to collect and explain the origin, history, and significance of both the liturgical and popular customs and celebrations that have grown in the course of many centuries around the observance of a great feast—in fact, the greatest one—of Christianity.

The Christmas Book has been most graciously received. May this little companion work find the same friendly and kind reception, and may it help to deepen not only the understanding but also the fruitful celebration of the sacred seasons of Lent, Holy Week, and Easter.

FRANCIS X. WEISER, S.J.

Weston College
Weston, Massachusetts

Contents

Notes on Chapter Illustrations

TO EMMANUEL COLLEGE

The First Easter

The world-conquering Romans regarded death as the doorway to oblivion, and future life as the dream of a bygone age. In A.D. 33, however, when Roman legionaries in Jerusalem were witnessing three crucified men in their last agony, something happened that shattered their cold complacency and awakened a vision in one of them. When the Man who was outstretched on the central cross died in the early afternoon, the sun suddenly darkened its face, the rocks split in crevices, the earth quaked, and the curtain of the temple was rent. Gazing at the lifeless victim, the Roman centurion cried out: "Truly this man was the Son of God."

11

Mere man could die, crucified for a cause; but only the God-man could rise from the dead. Christ had foretold He would arise on the third day. Would He be able to redeem this prophecy in fact, and thus give undeniable proof of His claim to divinity? Years later Saint Paul dared to assert: "If Christ has not risen, vain then is our preaching, vain too is your faith" (1 Cor. 15, 14).

It was in the pre-dawn of the third day, while sentinels kept their station at the tomb, that Our Lord emerged triumphantly from the sealed sepulcher to appear in regal glory to His faithful followers. His message of peace and consolation comforted forever the holy women who had come to anoint His body. The angelic herald stood before the empty tomb and declared: "Do not be afraid; for I know that you seek Jesus, who was crucified. He is not here, for He has risen even as He said. Come, see the place where the Lord was laid. And go quickly and tell His disciples that He has risen" (Matt. 28, 5-7).

This was the message that was too dark for Greece and too daring for Rome, until the Apostle of the Gentiles preached the Gospel of the Risen Redeemer: "Christ has risen from the dead, the first-fruits of those who have fallen asleep. For since by a man came death, by a man also comes resurrection of the dead. For as in Adam all die, so in Christ all will be made to live" (1 Cor. 15, 20-22). When the Roman Empire, which claimed to be immortal, sealed its doom in a day of barbarian invasions, the Mystical Body of Christ survived, and spread in deathless glory.

The Middle Ages, inheriting the Christian tradition, kept alive the celebration of Christ's Resurrection, or Easter, as the supreme festive day of the year-long liturgy. Reliving the Passion of Christ in the forty days of Lent and especially in Holy Week, the faithful endeavored to relive also His Resurrection in their own lives.

Christian churches observe their seasons in a different manner from the rest of the world. January is the beginning of the calendar year which is reckoned in months and days of the month, while the Church begins her year with Advent (in preparation for Christmas), and computes it by the important events in Our Lord's life.

It is a fact that millions of Christians in our time are becoming more and more interested in liturgy and in the true meaning of the Lenten season as a preparation for a happy Easter. The climax of all liturgy is, of course, "the feast of feasts," Easter.

CHAPTER 1

Man and Nature

Just as many Christmas customs and similar observances had their origin in pre-Christian times, so,
too, some of the popular traditions of Lent and
Easter date back to ancient nature rites. The "spring
lore" of the Indo-European races is their source in
this case. From Yule to the summer solstice (which
was celebrated on June 24), a continuous tradition
of spring rites and symbolic fertility cults was practiced among our forefathers.[1]

The Fight against Winter · These activities began at
the winter solstice, when the day was shortest in the

15

year, and lasted until April or May. In order to frighten the demons of winter away, and at the same time to hide their own identity, the participants in this "fight" were disguised in wild and strange costumes. Wearing masks of horrible size and shape, they ran shouting and screaming through the open spaces around their homes.

Mummers' and carnival masquerades of later times, and the uproarious celebrations on various days between Christmas and Easter have their origin in this "fight." In southern Germany, in Austria, and among the Slavic nations such mummers' (*Perchten*) parades are still held every year. Dressed in ancient costumes and masks, the paraders follow traditional routes, accompanied by the loud and discordant noise of drums, cowbells, crude trumpets, and the cracking of whips or the shooting of mortars (*Böller*).

Another rite of "frightening the winter away" was the setting of fires between Yule and May. Attached to wooden rings or wheels, brands were sent rolling down the meadows from the hilltops. In southern Germany the first Sunday of Lent is still called *Brandsonntag* (Fire Sunday), when many such burning wheels move, sparkling in the dark night, on the hillsides and from the mountain peaks. In France the same Sunday was called *Fête des brandons* (Feast of

Torches) because on that day young people ran through the streets with firebrands to chase the winter away.

As the spring advanced and green patches of new grass appeared, as days grew warmer, the people celebrated "winter's burial." Sometimes with mock sadness, more often, however, with wild and joyous abandon, they dragged a ragged straw figure, often of giant size, through the village, accompanied by a large crowd of "mourners" in masquerade. Popular funeral rites were held, and the huge figure, dressed in white to symbolize the snow, was either buried or "executed" by quartering, drowning, burning, or hanging, with the lusty approval and acclaim of the onlookers. In the sixteenth century they started in many places to stuff the figure with powder and fireworks, so that the heat of the flames would make it explode with a thunderous crash.

Such burials of winter are still held in many countries. Very often, however, the ceremony has come to be interpreted as the "burial of carnival," or the "burning of Judas" on Holy Saturday.

The climax of these rites was the play depicting "winter's defeat." The actors, impersonating with appropriate dress the figures of summer and winter, would carry on a verbal battle in which winter, de-

17

feated, conceded the victory to summer. Here is the ancient text of such a scene, as it is still performed in rural sections of Austria (S: Summer, W: Winter):

S:　When I across the meadow walk,
　　There are blossoms and flowers on every stalk.
　　O sir, o mine, the summer is fine.

W:　When I across the meadow go,
　　The streams are ice, and all is snow.
　　O sir, o mine, the winter is fine.

S:　In the summer time, on harvest day,
　　I give you wheat and fruit and hay.
　　O sir, o mine, the summer is fine.

W:　Your harvest will do nobody good,
　　Unless the winter stores your food.
　　O sir, o mine, the winter is fine.

S:　O winter, you wild and ravenous cheat,
　　You devour my wood and steal my heat.
　　O sir, o mine, the summer is fine.

W:　O summer, I need no wood nor stone,
　　I build me bridges of ice alone.
　　O sir, o mine, the winter is fine.

S:　O winter, thy bridges do not last;
　　I melt them, and all thy power is past.
　　O sir, o mine, the summer is fine.

W: O summer, I must admit you are right:
      You are my lord, and I am your knight.

Both: O sir, o mine, the *summer* is fine.[2]

Fertility Rites · While the struggle between summer
and winter went on (December to April), many symbolic celebrations were held to demonstrate how
anxious people were for the coming warm season and
to insure as well the blessings of fertility (the important second part of these ancient rites).

The joy over the appearance of new plants and
flowers in spring prompted man to attribute to them
a special power of protection and healing. People
planted special spring flower gardens; they brought
branches of early-blossoming plants, like pussy willows, into their homes; they decorated themselves
and their living rooms with wreaths of flowers and
clusters of blossoms. A striking Christian variation
of these nature rites was the medieval custom of
planting "Mary gardens," which were made up of all
the flowers and herbs that are ascribed by love and
legend as a special tribute to the Blessed Virgin. This
charming and inspiring tradition has been revived
in many places in Europe and more recently in this
country.[3]

In a typical Mary garden the statue of the Madonna occupies a place of honor, either in the center

19

or in a grotto against the wall, with, usually, a bird-
bath or bubbling fountain built in front of it. Some of
the more familiar plants of the many that belong in
a typical Mary garden are:

Columbine and *Trefoil* are said to have sprung forth
at the touch of Mary's foot, and consequently bear the
popular names Our Lady's shoes or Our Lady's slippers.

Marigold (Mary's bud) has bell-shaped blossoms of
vivid yellow. An old legend says, "Her dresses were
adorned with Marigold." This flower was used to decorate her shrines for the Feast of the Annunciation (March
25) and during the month of May.

Lily-of-the-valley (Our Lady's tears). This delicate
flower is still widely used in Germany, where it is called
Maiglöckchen (May bells), to decorate the Mary shrines
in churches and homes during the Virgin's month (May).

Foxgloves thrive in moist and shaded places; they blossom in many colors and present a most attractive sight
with their clusters of little bells, which were called Our
Lady's thimbles in medieval times.

Snowdrop. This charming flower is the first herald of
spring in Europe. It often blossoms as early as Candlemas
(February 2) between patches of melting snow; hence
the name. In Germany it is called "Snow bell" (*Schnee-
glöcklein*). Little bouquets of snowdrops are the first
floral tribute of the year at the shrines of the Madonna
on Candlemas. It is a popular emblem of Mary's radiant
purity and of her freedom from any stain of sin.

Lily. This stately and dignified flower has been associated from ancient times with Jesus and Mary, and is called Madonna lily in many parts of Europe. At Easter its brilliant and fragrant blossoms symbolize the radiance of the Lord's risen life. Later in the year it is used to decorate the shrines of Mary, especially on July 2, the Feast of the Visitation. It also is an old and traditional symbol of innocence, purity, and virginity.

Rosemary produces delicate and fragrant blossoms of pale blue color in early spring. According to legend, the plant originally bloomed in white; however, it turned blue (Mary's color) in reward for the service it offered when Our Lady looked for some bush on which to spread her Child's tiny garments after having washed them on the way to Egypt. The bushes do not grow very tall but as they grow older they spread out and thicken, forming a dense bush. There is an old superstition that "the rosemary passeth not commonly the height of Christ when he was on earth."

Violets are dedicated to Mary as symbols of her humility. They are said to have blossomed forth outside her window when she spoke the words, "Behold, I am a handmaid of the Lord." Leaving her, the angel of God blessed the little flowers in passing, thus endowing them with the tenderest and most beautiful fragrance of all plants.

Roses were associated with Mary from early times. Saint Dominic (1221) is credited with the spreading of the familiar devotion called the "Rosary (*rosarium*) of the Blessed Virgin Mary." The word "rosary" originally

21

meant a rose garden but was later used in the sense of "rose garland." Three colors are especially consecrated to Mary: white roses as symbols of her joys, red roses as emblems of her sufferings, and yellow (golden) roses as heralds of her glories.

Another fertility rite was the symbolic "plowing" of the earth in early spring, with a real plow or a wooden log, to make the soil fertile. It was done with elaborate ceremonies, often connected with a mummers' parade. In Germany and eastern Europe it became a part of the carnival celebration (*Blochziehen*). In England it was held in January, and the Monday after Epiphany (January 6) acquired from this ancient custom the name "Ploughmonday." The original fertility cult is still preserved in the superstition that maidens who draw the plow or sit on it or touch it will soon be married and will be blessed with healthy offspring.

Chemistry and physics as we know them, of course, were a mystery to our pre-Christian forefathers. From constant observation, however, they knew only too well the effects of rain, or lack of rain, on vegetation and life. Water, therefore, assumed in their minds a magic role of producing fertility, health, and new life. This is the basis of the many ancient "water rites." It was the fashion among all nations of Europe to sprinkle women and girls with water, thus to insure them the blessings of fertility and good health. This custom is still preserved in European countries, where during carnival time or at Easter the boys sprinkle or splash water on the girls, and the girls retaliate on the following day.

In the Middle Ages the Feast of Christ's Resurrection became the favorite time for such ancient water rites. In many parts of central and eastern Europe, and also in France, girls and women wash their faces in brooks and rivers on Easter Sunday morning (*Osterwaschen*). It is a widespread legend that on Easter Day all running water is especially blessed because the Risen Lord sanctified all life-giving elements and bestowed upon them special powers for the one great day of His Resurrection.

Similar customs prevail in French Canada, where people wash themselves with water taken from rivers or fountains on Easter Sunday. They also preserve it in bottles, and it is said to remain fresh until the following Easter, being credited with great healing powers. In Germany and Austria bridegroom and bride sprinkle each other with such water before going to church on their wedding day. Domestic animals, too, are believed to benefit from the power of Easter water. In many parts of Europe farmers sprinkle them with water drawn from brooks or springs during Easter night. In some sections of Germany horses are ridden into a river on Easter Sunday to obtain for them protection and good health. Irish legends attribute to water fetched on Easter Day magic powers against witches and evil spirits.

Among the Slavic nations the men in rural districts will rise at midnight on Holy Thursday and walk to the nearest brook to wash themselves. They do this in honor and imitation of Christ who, according to an old Oriental legend, fell into the river Cedron on His way to the Passion.

The Church has provided a Christian version of the ancient water rite by blessing and distributing Easter water on Holy Saturday, thus elevating the pre-Christian symbolism of nature into a Christian sacramental. It is customary for millions the world over to obtain for their households the Easter water blessed on Holy Saturday.

Another rite of fertility was the touch with the "rod of life" (*Lebensrute*). A few branches were broken from a young bush, and any youth or maiden touched or hit by this rod was believed to obtain the blessings of health and fertility. This symbolism was incorporated in the mysteries of the Roman goddess Libera, in which young matrons were initiated into childbearing and motherhood by a ritual of flagellation to insure fertility.

All through Europe this custom is found at carnival time or Eastertide. Girls and women are tapped with leaved rods or pussy willow branches, which are often decorated with flowers and ribbons. A familiar relic of this tradition seems to be the modern practice of throwing the bridal bouquet at weddings. It reveals its ancient symbolism by the claim that the girl who catches the bouquet (thus being touched by the rod of life) will be the next one to marry.

The greater part of the pre-Christian usage and meaning of the rod of life was transferred in medieval times to the Christian symbolism of the "palms" which the Church blesses on Palm Sunday.

When the victory of spring was fully won and winter had disappeared, our forefathers used to celebrate a joyous "spring festival" by dancing around a gaily decorated tree (maypole), cleared of branches except on its top. The tree itself was a symbol of nature's triumph, a tribute to the power of new life. In medieval times maypoles were erected in every community. In rural towns of the Austrian Tyrol the inhabitants still observe the appealing custom of planting a maypole, at any time of the year, in front of houses where newly wed couples live; there the gay symbol remains until the night after the birth of the first child, when the young men of the village silently take it down.

It may come as a surprise to many to learn that the crowning of the "May Queen" is another ancient rite which has been practiced by Indo-European peoples for thousands of years. One of the girls, chosen by a vote of young men, was led in procession to the place of the spring festival, where she presided over the celebration. She was often accompanied by a young man who was called the May King. Both were dressed in festive robes, wore wreaths of flowers on their heads, and held in their hands a wooden scepter (the rod of life) adorned with flowers and ribbons.

The final victory over winter was also celebrated with the setting of "bonfires" on hills and mountain peaks in all countries of northern Europe during pre-Christian times. The Easter fires and Saint John's fires are still a cherished part of the annual folklore in many sections, especially the Alpine provinces.

Thus the religious celebration of the sacred seasons of Lent and Easter is accompanied by many popular traditions of ancient origin which have added a charming touch to the supernatural meanings of the season. Under the guiding inspiration of the Church a popular observance was molded, in which most of the natural customs were ennobled through the spiritual power of Christianity.

CHAPTER 2

Farewell to Alleluia

Alleluia, or *hallelujah,* is one of the few Hebrew words adopted by the Christian Church from apostolic times. It means "Praise the Lord!"

On Saturday before Septuagesima Sunday (the third Sunday before Lent) this ancient and hallowed exclamation of joy and praise in the Christian liturgy is officially discontinued in the Western Church to signify the approach of the solemn season of Lent. According to the regulation of Pope Alexander II (1073) the Alleluia is sung twice after the prayers of the Divine Office,[4] and not heard again till the solemn vigil service of Easter, when it once more is used as a glorious proclamation of Easter joy. The Greek Church, however, still retains the Alleluia even in Lent.

Saint John the Evangelist mentioned alleluia in his Apocalypse (chapter 19), and the early Church accepted the word from the beginning. From Jerusalem the custom of using it spread with the expanding Church into all nations. It is interesting to note that nowhere and at no time was any effort made to translate it into the vernacular, as Saint Isidor of Seville (636) mentioned in his writings.[5] He explains it by the reverence for the hallowed traditions of the Apostolic Church.

In addition to the official liturgy, as early as the third century, the Christian writer Tertullian said in his treatise on prayer, the faithful of his time used to insert many alleluias in their private devotions.[6] Saint Jerome (420) praised the pious farmers and tradesmen who used to sing it at their toil, and the mothers who taught their babies to pronounce alleluia before any other word.[7]

In the Roman Empire the Alleluia became the favorite prayerful song of oarsmen and navigators. Saint Augustine (430) alluded to this custom, saying, "Let the Alleluia be our sweet rowing-song!"[8] And some years later, the Roman poet and bishop Sidonius Apollinaris (480) described how the river banks and shores of Gaul resounded with the Alleluia song of the rowing boatmen.[9] Even the Roman soldiers fighting against pagan barbarians used it as battle cry and war song. Saint Bede the Venerable (735), in his history of England, reported such an "Alleluia victory" won by the Christian Bretons over the Picts and Scots in 429.[10]

Finally, the expression "Alleluia, the Lord is risen" became the general greeting of Christians in early medieval times on the Feast of the Resurrection. Apart from these popular usages the Alleluia has at all times found its primary and most meaningful application in the official liturgy. In the early centuries, the Roman Church used it only during Easter time, but it soon spread over the rest of the ecclesiastical year, except of course, during Lent. In many places it was sung even at funerals and burial Masses as an expression of the conviction that for a true Christian the day of death was actually the birthday of eternal life, a day of joy.[11]

The *depositio* (discontinuance) of the Alleluia on the eve of Septuagesima assumed in medieval times a solemn and emotional note of saying farewell to the beloved song. Despite the fact that Pope Alexander II had ordered a very simple and somber way of "deposing" the Alleluia, a variety of farewell customs prevailed in many countries up to the sixteenth

29

century. They were inspired by the sentiment which Bishop William Duranti (1296) voiced in his commentaries on the Divine Office: "We part from the Alleluia as from a beloved friend, whom we embrace many times and kiss on mouth, head and hand, before we leave him." [12]

The liturgical office on the eve of Septuagesima was performed in many churches with special solemnity, and alleluias were freely inserted in the sacred text, even to the number of twenty-eight final alleluias in the Church of Auxerre (France). This custom also inspired some tender poems which were sung or recited during Vespers in honor of the sacred word. The best known of these hymns is, *Alleluia, dulce carmen* (Alleluia, Song of Gladness), composed by an unknown author of the tenth century. It was translated into English by John Mason Neale (1866) and may be found in the official hymnal of the Protestant Episcopal Church.[13] Here is another translation, of three stanzas, from the Latin text:

> Alleluia, hymn of sweetness,
>   Hallowed word, eternal song.
> Alleluia, praise and prayer
>   Offered by the angels' throng,
> Ringing through the realm of Glory,
>   Ever new and ever strong.

Alleluia, now no longer
    Will be heard on earth below.
Alleluia, sin and sorrow
    Interrupt thy gracious flow;
Lent is come and we, the sinners,
    Humbly must our penance show.

Hear, o God, the plea of mercy,
    Father, Son and Holy Ghost:
Through a blessed Easter help us
    So to live that, last and most,
We may sing the Alleluia
    Evermore in Heaven's host.

In some French churches the custom developed
in ancient times of allowing the congregation to
take part in the celebration of a quasi-liturgical farewell ceremony. The clergy abstained from any role
in this popular service. Choirboys officiated in their
stead at what was called "Burial of the Alleluia" performed the Saturday afternoon before Septuagesima
Sunday. We find a description of it in the fifteenth-
century statute book of the Church of Toul:

On Saturday before Septuagesima Sunday all choir boys
gather in the sacristy during the prayer of the None, to
prepare for the burial of the Alleluia. After the last
Benedicamus [*i.e.*, at the end of the service] they march
in procession, with crosses, tapers, holy water and cen-

sers; and they carry a coffin, as in a funeral. Thus they
proceed through the aisle, moaning and mourning, until
they reach the cloister. There they bury the coffin; they
sprinkle it with holy water and incense it; whereupon
they return to the sacristy by the same way.[14]

In Paris, a straw figure bearing in golden letters
the inscription "Alleluia" was carried out of the
choir at the end of the service and burned in the
church yard.

With the exception of these quaint aberrations,
however, the farewell to alleluia in most countries
was an appropriate addition to the official ceremonies
of the liturgy. The special texts (hymns, responsories,
antiphons) used on that occasion were taken mostly
from Holy Scripture, and are filled with pious senti-
ments of devotion, like the following unusual per-
sonification collected from a farewell service of the
Mozarabic liturgy of Spain (ninth or tenth century):

> Stay with us today, Alleluia,
>   And tomorrow thou shalt part.
> When the morning rises,
>   Thou shalt go thy way.
> Alleluia, alleluia.
>
> May the Lord be thy custodian, Alleluia,
>   And the angel of God accompany thee.

May the Lord keep thee alive
  And protect thee from every evil.
Alleluia, alleluia.

The mountains and hills shall rejoice, Alleluia,
  While they await thy glory.
Thou goest, Alleluia; may thy way be blessed,
  Until thou shalt return with joy.
Alleluia, alleluia, alleluia.[15]

Thus the Alleluia is sung for the last time and not
heard again until it suddenly bursts into glory during
the Mass of the Easter Vigil. No one who has witnessed it will ever forget the deep emotions of peace
and Easter joy that surge up in the hearts and show
on the faces of the faithful when the celebrant of the
Mass on Holy Saturday intones this sacred word,
repeating it three times, as a jubilant herald of the
Resurrection of Christ. And Christian Churches all
over the world include the Alleluia in all their Easter
services in praise of the Risen Lord. This word also
inspired Handel's familiar "Hallelujah Chorus" in his
oratorio *The Messiah* (1742).

CHAPTER 3

Pre-Lent and Carnival

The three Sundays preceding Lent are called Septuagesima (seventieth), Sexagesima (sixtieth), and
Quinquagesima (fiftieth). Actually they are *not* the
seventieth, sixtieth, and fiftieth days before Easter
as their names would indicate. These titles seem to
have been arbitrarily chosen for the sake of round
numbers, in keeping with the much older term of
Quadragesima (fortieth) which denotes the first Sunday of Lent.

The preparatory time of pre-Lent was established
by the practice of the Greek Church, which started
its great fast earlier than the Roman Church did. We

34

find the pre-Lenten Sundays mentioned as early as 541, in the fourth Council of Orleans. At the time of Pope Saint Gregory I (604) they were already celebrated in Rome with the same liturgical Mass texts that are used today.

The spirit of pre-Lent is one of penance, devotion, and atonement, the Sunday Masses and the liturgical rules reflecting this character. The Gloria is omitted, purple vestments are worn, and the altars may no longer be decorated with flowers.

In ancient times, when the law of abstinence was much stricter and included many other foods besides meat, the clergy and a good number of the laity started abstaining progressively during the pre-Lenten season, until they entered the complete fast on Ash Wednesday. After Quinquagesima (*i.e.*, the last Sunday *before* Lent) this voluntary fasting began with abstinence from meat; consequently, this Sunday was called *Dominica carnevala* (Farewell-to-meat Sunday), from which comes the word "carnival." Another, more scholarly, explanation of the derivation of carnival is that it comes from the Latin *Carnem levare* (*carnelevarium*) which means "withdrawal" or "removal" of meat.

The Oriental Church, too, abstained first from meat, but began on Sexagesima (the second Sunday before Lent), which is called "Meatless" (*apokreo*,

35

in Greek; *miasopust,* in Slavic). With Quinquagesima the Eastern Church began (and still begins) the abstinence from butter, cheese, milk, and eggs. Thus in eastern Europe that day is called "Cheeseless Sunday" (*syropust*).

In preparation for Lent the faithful in medieval times used to go to confession on Tuesday before Ash Wednesday. From this practice, that day became known as "Shrove Tuesday" (the day on which people are shriven from sins). An old English sermon of the eleventh century exhorts the faithful thus: "In the week immediately before Lent, everyone shall go to his confessor; and his confessor shall so shrive him as he then may hear by his deeds what he is to do." [16]

A worldly aspect of pre-Lent is the familiar celebration known since medieval times by the term "carnival." Carnival celebrations are still held in central Europe and among the Latin nations of Europe and America. The German word for this time of celebration, *Fassnacht,* or *Fasching,* comes from the ancient *vasen,* which means "running around crazily," and was adopted by the Slavic nations (*fasiangy*) and by the Hungarians (*farsang*). Another German word of later origin is *Fastnacht* (Eve of the Fast). The Lithuanians call this season *Uzgavenes* (pre-Lent).

36

What is the origin of the modern carnival celebration? As the names indicate, there are various causes, but the primary reason for this sort of carnival is the feasting, rejoicing, and reveling preceding the imminent season of fast and abstinence. It is a trait of human nature to anticipate approaching privations by greater or lesser excesses. The intensity of this urge, however, should not be judged to stem from the mild Lenten laws of today but from the strict and harsh observance of ancient times, which makes modern man shiver at the mere knowledge of its details. No wonder the good people of past centuries felt entitled to "have a good time" before they started on their awesome fast.

Another reason for the feasting, and a very practical one, was the necessity for finishing those foods which could not be eaten during Lent, and which, in fact, could not even be kept in homes during the fast—meat, butter, cheese, milk, eggs, fats, and bacon. This meant an increased consumption of rich foods and pastries the week before Ash Wednesday. Hence have come the names "Fat Tuesday" (*Fetter Dienstag*, in German; *Mardi gras* in French); "Butter Week" (*Sedmica syrnaja*) in Russia and other Slavic countries; and "Fat Days" (*Tluste Dni*) in Poland.

In the northern counties of England, the Monday of carnival week is "Collop Monday" (from the Latin

37

colpones, cut pieces). Collops are eaten in every house, and consist of sliced meat or bacon, mixed with eggs, and fried in butter. In Scotland people eat "Crowdie," a kind of porridge cooked with butter and milk. On Tuesday, England enjoys her famous Shrove Tuesday pancakes. The Germans have pastries called *Fassnachtstollen,* the Austrians *Faschingskrapfen.*

Fastelavnsboller are sold in Norway in great quantities during carnival time. Resembling our muffins, these "bollers" are sold throughout the whole year plain, but at carnival time they are filled with whipped cream and coated with sugar and frosting. Quinquagesima Sunday is there called *Fastelavnssondag.*

Of the northern countries, Russia, before the present regime, attached a national and strictly regulated importance to the several seasons of carnival, Lent, and Easter. Carnival or "Butter Week" was a general holiday. As in the western countries, there are pre-Christian relics in the Russian festival too, but these relics often present an extraordinary blending of Scandinavian and Asiatic myths. In the country districts a fantastic figure called *Masslianitsa* (Butter Goddess) is gaily decorated and driven about on a sledge while the peasants sing special songs and *horovode* (folk choruses). At the end of the week

38

it is burned, and a formal farewell is bidden to pleasure until Easter. Rich but unsweetened pancakes (*blinni*) are served in every household at carnival time.

Since carnival was a time of feasting and reveling, it was only natural that many elements of the pre-Christian spring lore should have become part of the celebration. Lent excluded the boisterous practices of mumming and masquerading, so what better time could be found for it than the gay days of the carnival? All the familiar features of our modern carnival celebrations are firmly rooted in a tradition that actually dates from about the fourteenth century.

It has often been claimed that the pre-Christian element of the carnival frolics is a growth of the revels of the Roman "Saturnalia," a pagan feast in honor of the field god Saturnus held annually in December. It is true that the Saturnalia contained some features similar to our carnival. This similarity, however, is no proof of direct connection, since both festivals, independent of each other, could have adopted customs and rites from the much older Indo-European spring lore. In fact, modern research reveals that the pre-Christian parts of the carnival celebration have come down to us through the folklore of the Germanic and Slavic races rather than from Greece or Rome.

39

The popes, as temporal rulers of their state, acknowledged the carnival practice in Rome by regulating its observance, correcting its abuses, and providing entertainment for the masses. Paul II (1471) started the famous horse races which gave the name *Corso* to one of Rome's ancient streets, the former *Via Lata* (broad street). He also introduced the carnival pageants for which the Holy City was famous. Within the past few centuries other cities, too, have developed their own special features of carnival celebration, like the famed carnival of Cologne, the parade of gondolas in Venice, the carnival balls of Vienna, the floats and parades in the cities of South America, and the mummers' parade in Philadelphia. The best-known celebration of carnival in America is the famous Mardi Gras in New Orleans, which takes its name from the day on which it is annually held. Similar celebrations are also held on that day in other cities and towns of Louisiana, Florida, and Alabama. In the last state, and in several cities of Florida and Louisiana, including New Orleans, the day is a legal holiday. It cannot be said, perhaps, that the participants in these revelries make up for their excesses by anything like the ancient or even modern fast and penance during the Lenten season, which begins on the next day, Ash Wednesday.

A detailed description of carnival, both ancient

40

and modern, would fill a volume. What could easily be a time of good-natured and harmless enjoyment unfortunately has been turned by many into a wild orgy of eating, drinking, and other excesses. The carnival celebrations of modern big cities have not improved the standard of the "dark ages" very much. At a recent carnival in Rio de Janeiro, Brazil, seventeen people died in street fights and other accidents, and five thousand persons required medical treatment for injuries received.[17]

For years civic and religious authorities have fought this trend, generally with little effect. Pope Pius V (1590) imposed harsh punishments on offenders during the carnival seasons in Rome; he went so far as to erect whipping posts in conspicuous places as a caution and warning. In the city of Vienna it was found necessary, in 1654, to issue a municipal edict carrying threat of arrest and heavy fines for "lascivious behavior and the carrying of weapons" at carnival time. Such prohibitions had to be repeated almost every year during the seventeenth and eighteenth centuries, until finally the carnival masquerades were completely suppressed in the streets of the Austrian capital, and only allowed as indoor amusements at the carnival balls, where people danced to the strains of Johann Strauss's waltzes.

In order to offset the many scandals committed

41

at carnival time, Pope Benedict XIV, in 1748, instituted a special devotion for the three days preceding
Lent, called "Forty Hours of Carnival," which is held
in many churches of Europe and America, in places
where carnival frolics are of general and long-stand-
ing tradition.

CHAPTER 4

Sackcloth and Ashes

Lent is a fast of forty days, not including Sundays, beginning with Ash Wednesday and ending with the Saturday before Easter Sunday. It is a period set aside by the Church for fasting and self-denial in token of our Lord's fasting for forty days and forty nights before His temptation. Pope Gregory I (604) described Lent as "the spiritual tithing of the year."

The first day of Lent is called "Ash Wednesday" in all Christian countries of the Western world from the ceremony of imposing blessed ashes in the form of a cross on the foreheads of the faithful while the priest pronounces the words, *"Memento homo quia*

43

pulvis es et in pulverem reverteris" (Remember, man, that thou art dust, and to dust thou shalt return) (Gen. 3, 19). The name Ash Wednesday (*Feria quarta cinerum*) was officially introduced by Pope Urban II (1099); prior to that the first day of Lent was called "Beginning of the Fast" (*initium jejunii*).

The ashes used are obtained from burning the blessed palms of the previous Palm Sunday. They are also given a special blessing before being distributed on Ash Wednesday. The four prayers employed in the Roman Missal for this ceremony date back to the eighth century. Here is the first prayer, which contains the actual rite of blessing:

Almighty and eternal God, have mercy on the penitent sinners, forgive those who humbly ask remission; and deign to send thy holy Angel from Heaven, to bless and sanctify these ashes. May they constitute a wholesome remedy for all who implore thy holy name in humility and accuse themselves sincerely of their sins; who deplore their misdeeds in the sight of thy Divine pity, or who appeal in anxious supplication to thy exceeding kindness. Through the invocation of thy holy name, grant that all those, on whom these ashes will be imposed for the remission of sins, may also obtain health of the body and protection of their souls. Through Christ our Lord. Amen.

The use of ashes as a token of penance and sorrow is an ancient one, often mentioned in the Scripture of the Old Testament (Jonas 3, 5-9; Jeremias 6, 26 and 25, 34; etc.). Christ, too, refers to this custom, in Matthew 11, 21. The Church accepted it from Jewish tradition and preserved its original meaning. The early Christian writer Tertullian (third century) mentions the imposition of ashes as one of the external marks of Christian penance.[18] Persons who had committed serious public sin and scandal were enjoined on Ash Wednesday with the practice of "public penance." The period of this penance lasted until Holy Thursday when they were solemnly reconciled, absolved from their sins, and allowed to receive Holy Communion. Since it extended through forty days, its observance was called "quarantine" (forty). This word was also accepted into general use to denote a separation or expulsion from human contact in the case of infectious diseases.

The imposition of public penance on Ash Wednesday was an official rite in Rome as early as the fourth century; and soon spread to all Christianized nations. Numerous descriptions of this ancient ceremony have been preserved in medieval manuscripts and, in every detail, breathe a spirit of harshness and humility really frightening to us of the present generation.

Public sinners approached their priests shortly

45

before Lent to accuse themselves of their misdeeds, and were presented by the priests on Ash Wednesday to the bishop of the place. Outside the cathedral, poor and noble alike stood barefoot, dressed in sackcloth, heads bowed in humble contrition. The bishop, assisted by his canons, assigned to each one particular acts of penance according to the nature and gravity of his crime. Whereupon they entered the church, the bishop leading one of them by the hand, the others following in single file, holding each other's hands. Before the altar, not only the penitents, but also the bishop and all his clergy recited the seven penitential psalms.[19] Then, as each sinner approached, the bishop imposed his hands on him, sprinkled him with holy water, threw the blessed ashes on his head, and invested him with the hair shirt. Finally he admonished ("with tears and sighs" as the regulation suggests): "Behold you are cast out from the sight of holy mother Church because of your sins and crimes, as Adam the first man was cast out of Paradise because of his transgression."

After this ceremony the penitents were led out of the church and forbidden to re-enter until Holy Thursday (for the solemn rite of reconciliation). Meanwhile they would spend Lent apart from their families in a monastery or some other place of voluntary confinement, where they occupied themselves

46

with prayer, manual labor, and works of charity. Among other things they had to go barefoot all through Lent, were forbidden to converse with others, were made to sleep on the ground or on a bedding of straw, and were unable to bathe or cut their hair.

Such was the public penance (in addition to the general Lenten fast) for "ordinary" cases of grave sin and scandal. The exact details of this penitential rite were not observed universally in the same manner, however, but varied according to time and place. For especially shocking and heinous crimes a much longer term was imposed. An ancient manuscript records the case of an English nobleman of the eleventh century who received a penance of seven years for notorious crimes and scandals committed. The duties of his first year of public penance consisted of the following details: He must not bear arms (a bitter humiliation for a nobleman of that time!); he must not receive Holy Communion except in danger of death; he must not enter the church to attend Mass but remain standing outside the church door; he must eat very sparingly, taking meat only on Sundays and major feasts; on three days of the week he must abstain from wine; he must feed one poor person every day from what he would have spent on himself. The document closes with the words: "If, however, thou shalt have borne this penance willingly for one year, in the future with God's grace thou shalt be judged more leniently." [20]

These examples will make clearer, perhaps, what an indulgence granted by the Church means in our time. An indulgence of seven years is the remission of temporal punishment for sins already forgiven to the extent of a seven years' personal penance such as just described.

Although the imposition of ashes originally applied only to public sinners, many devout people soon voluntarily submitted to it, so that by the end of the eleventh century it had become general in all European countries. The popes, too, adopted it for their personal use. In medieval times they walked barefoot on Ash Wednesday to the church of Santa Sabina, accompanied by their cardinals (also barefoot), where they all received the ashes from the hands of the Grand Penitentiary.

After the Reformation, the imposition of ashes was discontinued in most Protestant churches, but was kept alive for a time in the Church of England by special proclamations of the government in 1538 and 1550 which reaffirmed it. It was gradually neglected, and completely forgotten in England by the seventeenth century. Today the Anglican Church keeps a relic of the ancient character of Ash Wednesday in

48

a special service of "Commination," a solemn avowal of God's anger and justice against sinners. In recent years, some Protestant churches have returned to the practice of imposing ashes.

Among the members of the Oriental Churches, Ash Wednesday is not observed. Their Lent begins on Monday before Ash Wednesday, which they call "Clean Monday" because the faithful not only cleanse their souls in penance but also wash and scrub their cooking utensils very thoroughly to remove all traces of meat and fat for the penitential season.

An amusing story about Ash Wednesday may be found in the *Letters* of Ogier Ghislain de Busbecq (1592), ambassador of Emperor Ferdinand I at the court of Sultan Suleiman I. A certain Turkish official, he writes, traveled on a diplomatic mission through some European countries and observed the carnival revelries in one of them. Upon his return to Constantinople he reported to the sultan that at a certain time of the year the Christians in one of the countries went raving mad, but that a mysterious powder of ashes sprinkled on them by their priests would instantly restore them to sanity and heal them from all their madness.[21]

This might well be a tall tale, but it was taken very seriously by Pope Benedict XIV (1758), who quoted it, in ponderous Latin, in his encyclical (public letter

to all churches) about the abuses of carnival celebrations. In the same document the Pope told of the
many complaints he had received from bishops that
people who had reveled all night would appear in
church on Ash Wednesday morning still dressed in
their carnival costumes, remove the masks to receive
the ashes, then go home and spend the rest of the
day in bed to recover from their excesses.[22]

Even today the custom is practiced in some parts
of central Europe of burying the carnival in the early
hours before sunrise on Ash Wednesday. Straw figures
decorated with herrings are carried in a mock funeral
to some clearing in the forest and buried there in the
snow. In Lithuania a play is given on the eve of Ash
Wednesday in which a very fat figure (*Lasininis*)
and a very thin one (*Kanapinis*) go through the mo-
tions of a great struggle. The thin man, representing
Lent, wins the fight over his opponent, who imper-
sonates the carnival days, throws him to the ground,
puts his foot on him, thus indicating that the lush
days of carnival are over and Lent is about to com-
mence.

The beginning of Ash Wednesday in most countries, however, usually strikes a more religious tone.
In many towns of Austria and southern Germany,
Lent is announced at midnight by the solemn ringing
of church bells. Again the following morning bells

call the faithful to the ceremony of the ashes (*Einäscherung*). It is customary to take some of the blessed ashes home to put on the foreheads of sick relatives. In Bavaria, people who received the ashes in church touch foreheads with those at home who are not able to attend the service.

Another interesting symbol of penance in medieval times was the "Lenten Cloth," a common tradition in England, France, and Germany from the eleventh century on. In Germany it was also called by the popular name of "Hunger-Cloth" (*Hungertuch, Schmachtlappen*). It was composed of an immense piece of cloth suspended in front of the sanctuary, and parted in the middle, which symbolized the outcasting of the penitent congregation from the sight of the altar. It was purple or white in color and decorated with crosses or scenes from Christ's Passion, was drawn back only for the main parts of the Mass, and remained suspended all through Lent until the words were read in the Passion Gospel of Wednesday before Easter (Holy Week). "And the curtain of the temple was torn in the middle" (Luke 23, 45).

The German preacher Thomas Kirchmeyer (Naogeorgus), one of the early Lutheran writers, has left a good description of such curtains in his satire *Pammachius* (1539):

51

The statues and the pictures now
Are covered far and nigh
In every church; and from the walls,
From roof and ceilings high,
Hang long and painted linen cloths
Which grimly do declare
The wrath and anger of the Lord
And hungry Lenten fare.

In the first centuries after the persecutions in the Roman Empire, Lent was not only a time of fasting and public penance but also the annual season of "preparation for baptism." [23] Those who had proved themselves serious applicants and had received preliminary instructions for many months would be admitted to the baptismal rites at the beginning of Lent. While the details of this practice varied locally, it was everywhere a somewhat hard school for the catechumens (candidates for baptism). If they were married, they had to live in continence all through Lent. They were not allowed to bathe and had to keep a complete fast every day until sunset. Above all, however, they had to practice fervent prayer and sincere contrition for their past sins. Separated from the faithful, they stood in church at every service, weak from hunger, and constantly admonished by the bishop, "harshly scourged with regulations and catechetical instructions" as Saint Augustine observed.

Standing barefoot on old rags or goat skins (symbolizing the godless world), they were exorcized in a special ceremony at the start of Lent. The bishop would breathe on them with a hiss and utter the command addressed to the devil whose slaves they had been in idolatry: "Depart, thou accursed one!" At another ceremony, toward the end of Lent, they listened for the first time to the Apostolic Creed named *symbolum* (probably meaning handclasp; contract). Each candidate solemnly affirmed his belief in the sacred truths, and was then obliged to memorize the Creed, in order to "return the handclasp" (*reddere symbolum*) by public recitation on Holy Saturday.

A week later (usually on Palm Sunday), the bishop entrusted them with the sacred words of the Lord's Prayer, the "Our Father." Finally, on Holy Thursday, they interrupted the fast and took a welcome bath at the public bathhouses, which were still in use in Roman cities and towns. The rest of the ceremonies, familiar to many from the ritual of baptism, were performed at the solemn Easter vigil.

Of the music for Ash Wednesday, by far the most famous work is the magnificently dramatic *Emendemus in Melius* (Let Us Change to A Better Life) of Cristobal Morales (1553), one of the great Spanish masters. This responsory, sung during the imposition of ashes, presents the penitential text in a musical setting for mixed voices, while above the chorus tenors break in at intervals with the words "*Memento homo quia pulvis es . . .*" (Remember, man, that thou art dust . . .).

The Great Fast

From the time of the apostles the Church has singled out two days of the week for special observance: in honor of Christ's Resurrection, Sunday replaced the ancient Sabbath as the new "day of the Lord," while in memory of His death, Friday became a weekly day of fast. In addition, a strict two-day fast was kept from Good Friday to Easter Sunday by many early Christians who did not eat or drink at all during that period. The practice of this "Passion fast" was based on the Lord's word: "The days will come when the bridegroom shall be taken away from them, and then they will fast on that day" (Mark 2, 20).

Eventually, a longer period of fasting was introduced in preparation for Easter, although its observance varied widely in the early centuries. Some churches fasted only in Holy Week, others for two or more weeks. Sunday was always excepted from the fast (in the Eastern Churches, Saturday as well). During the third and fourth centuries most churches gradually adopted a forty days' fast, in imitation of Christ who had fasted forty days in the desert (Luke 4, 2). Saint Athanasius (373), Patriarch of Alexandria (Africa), after having traveled to Rome and over the greater part of the Roman Empire in Europe, wrote in the year 339 that "the whole world" fasted forty days.[24]

The official term of the forty days' fast, Quadragesima (fortieth), is first mentioned in the fifth canon (decree) of the Council of Nicaea (325), although its reference to Lent is not yet certain; at the time of Saint Gregory (sixth century), however, the word was clearly applied to the period of Lenten fast. The same word was also applied to the Sunday on which the fast began at that time (*i.e.*, first Sunday of Lent). In the seventh century the period of fasting was made to begin four days earlier by Pope Gregory in order to establish the exact number of forty days, and since that time Lent has begun on the Wednesday before Quadragesima Sunday. (Only the Diocese of Milan in Italy still adheres to the ancient custom of starting the fast four days later, on the first Monday in Lent.)

The names for Lent in all Latin countries come from the word *Quadragesima*. The Greek word for it is *Tessarakoste*, and the Slavonic, *Chetyridesnica*. Our English term refers to the season of the year, sometimes explained as coming from the old Anglo-Saxon, *Lengten-tide*, springtime, when the days are lengthening. The German *Fastenzeit* means "fasting time." The Hungarians call it the "great Fast" (*Nagy-böjt*), and in Arabic-speaking countries they say the "big Fast" (*Sawm al-Kabir*). The Christian population of Malta has adopted the Moslem term *Randan* for Lent.

One of the most ancient customs in the Church was the annual proclamation of the Easter date and the beginning of Lent. In the first centuries of the Christian era the astronomers of Alexandria enjoyed the distinction of being outstanding experts in calculating dates which depended on the course of heavenly bodies, so, the Council of Nicaea in A.D. 325 directed the Archbishop of Alexandria with their help to determine for the whole Church the dates of Lent and Easter. Easter was to be the first Sunday following the full moon that appears on or next after the vernal equinox, about March 21. The date moves between March 22 and April 25. From 1916 to 1965 it occurs forty times in April and ten in March. Ash Wednesday, of course, is always forty days earlier.[25]

After receiving notification of the date, the Roman Pontiff proclaimed it to the rest of the Christian world, a ritual that has been preserved to our day in the form of pastoral letters which the bishops address every year shortly before Lent to their respective flocks. These are read from pulpits in parishes all over the world the Sunday before Lent and include the Lenten regulations for fast and abstinence.

How did the Christians fast in times past? The various forms of fast and abstinence in the first centuries made for confusion, but gradually there emerged general rules which eventually became the accepted practice of the whole Church. In a letter to Saint Augustine of Canterbury (604), Pope Saint Gregory the Great announced the final form of abstinence which soon became the law: "We abstain from flesh meat and from all things that come from flesh, as milk, cheese, eggs" (and butter, of course).[26] For almost a thousand years this remained the norm of abstinence for all except those who were excused for reasons of ill health. In fact, the Eastern Churches (and many pious people among the Slavic nations of the Latin Church) still keep their fast in this manner; they don't touch meat or eggs or butter all through Lent, not even on Sundays.

The observance of Lent also includes the *jejunium* (fast in the strict sense). Its early practice consisted in eating only once a day, toward evening; nothing else except a little water was taken all day. After the eighth century, the time for this one and only meal was advanced to the hour of the None in the liturgical prayer (meaning the ninth hour of the Roman day, which is three o'clock in the afternoon). This meal was gradually transferred to the middle of the day (hence our word "noon," from None). Emperor Charles the Great (814) ate his meal on fast days at two in the afternoon. The noonday meal did not become a general practice until the fourteenth century.

Saint Basil the Great (379), Archbishop of Caesaria in Asia Minor, vividly described in one of his sermons the widespread observance of the fast in the fourth century (and by "fasting" he meant only *one* meal a day):

There is no island, no continent, no city or nation, no distant corner of the globe, where the proclamation of Lenten fast is not listened to. Armies on the march and travelers on the road, sailors as well as merchants, all alike hear the announcement and receive it with joy.

Let no man then separate himself from the number of fasters, in which every race of mankind, every period of life, every class of society is included.[27]

The severity of the ancient rule was applied very sensibly at all times by the Church authorities. Saint John Chrysostom (407), Patriarch of Constantinople, gave this instruction: "If your body is not strong enough to continue fasting all day, no wise man will reprove you; for we serve a gentle and merciful Lord who expects nothing of us beyond our strength."[28] Pope Saint Leo I (461) pointed out that fasting is a means and not an end in itself; its purpose is to foster pure, holy, and spiritual activity. He coined the famous phrase which a thousand Christian writers have not ceased to reiterate: "What we forego by fasting is to be given as alms to the poor."[29]

It was not until the ninth century, however, that less rigid laws of fasting were introduced. It came about in 817 when the monks of the Benedictine order, who did much labor in the fields and on the farms, were allowed to take a little drink with a morsel of bread in the evening. This extremely light refreshment they took while they listened to the daily reading of the famous *Collationes* (collected instructions) written by the abbot Cassian in the fourth century. Our modern word "collation," meaning a slight repast, comes from this.

Eventually the Church extended the new laws to the laity as well, and by the end of medieval times they had become universal practice; everybody ate a light evening meal in addition to the main meal at noon. The present custom of taking some breakfast on fasting days is of very recent origin (beginning of the nineteenth century).

Abstinence from *lacticinia* (milk foods), which included milk, butter, cheese, and eggs, was never strictly enforced in Britain, Ireland, and Scandinavia because of the lack of oil and other substitute foods in those countries. The Church using common sense granted many dispensations in this matter in all countries of Europe. People who did eat the milk foods would often, when they could afford it, give alms for the building of churches or other pious endeavors. (One of the steeples of the Cathedral of Rouen in France is still known for this reason as "butter tower.") In the past centuries the Western Church increasingly allowed the consumption of *lacticinia*, or "white meats" as they were called, until the new code of Canon Law (1918) omitted them entirely from the list of abstinential foods.

During the Reformation some of the Protestant churches retained the Lenten fast, but not for long.

In England, the government issued a series of proclamations and statutes enjoining the duty of Lenten fast. It was announced by the town criers on order of Parliament and changed all the time. The Puritans substituted monthly fast days. After the Restoration (1660), the Lenten laws were generally neglected, although they remained on the statute book until 1863, when Parliament finally repealed them. On the other hand, while the observance of Lent was no longer kept, many members of the Protestant clergy (among them John Wesley) personally kept the fast and also recommended it to their congregations. The growth of the Oxford movement revived the practice of Lenten fasting in some Protestant groups, who now observe it according to the spirit of the universal Christian tradition.

Among the Eastern rites, many people still retain the old and strict routine, refusing to avail themselves of dispensations, although such are readily granted. In the Near East numerous priests keep a total fast for two days and eat only every third day all through Lent. Among the Russians, Ukrainians, and other Slavic nations, it is common practice to fast until three in the afternoon, while children, though not obliged to, fast voluntarily until noon. Among those sturdy farmers there are few people who cannot fast for reasons of health; they would be quite ashamed if they had to infringe on the full strictness of their traditions. In Ireland, too, many old people abstain from meat all through Lent.

The beginning of Lenten fast is celebrated with a touching ceremony in the Greek Church. The priests, wearing red vestments (which is the color of penance in the Orient), solemnly perform the Vespers on Quinquagesima Sunday, after which the congregation sings the ancient hymn "Hail Tranquil Light" (*Phos Hilaron*), as the illumination of the church is reduced to a minimum until Easter. As a preparation for the great fast clergy and people recite together the penitential prayer of Saint Ephrem the Syrian (373), which they accompany with prostrations and deep bowing:

O Lord and Ruler of Life, take from me the spirit of idleness, despair, cupidity, and empty talking.
But grant to thy servants the spirit of purity, meekness, patience and charity.
Yea, O Lord, grant that I may see my own sins and not judge my brother.
For thou art blessed for ever and ever. Amen.

After Vespers, the priests ask each other's pardon. So do the faithful, embracing each other. It is interesting to note that human forgiveness is never expressed; it is taken for granted. Instead, the expression is, "God will forgive you." And thus they go to bed, in peace and charity toward all men, awaking the next morning with renewed spirit to face the strictness of their sacred Lenten fast.

CHAPTER 6

Customs of Lent

Lenten Food · A most interesting survival of early Christian Lenten fare is a certain form of bread familiar to all of us. The Christians in the Roman Empire made a special dough consisting of flour, salt, and water only (since fat, eggs, and milk were forbidden). They shaped it in the form of two arms crossed in prayer, to remind them that Lent was a season of penance and devotion. They called these breads "little arms" (*bracellae*). From the Latin word the Germans later coined the term "*brezel*" or "*prezel*," from which comes our word "pretzel." The oldest known picture of a pretzel may be seen in

65

a manuscript from the fifth century in the Vatican.[30]

All through medieval times and into the present, pretzels remained an item of Lenten food in many parts of Europe. In Germany, Austria, and Poland, they made their annual appearance on Ash Wednesday; special vendors (*Brezelmann*) sold them on the streets of cities and towns. People would eat them for lunch, together with a stein of their mild, home-brew beer. In Poland they were eaten in beer soup.

In the cities pretzels were distributed to the poor on many days during Lent. In parts of Austria, children wore them suspended from the palm bushes on Palm Sunday. With the end of Lent the pretzels disappeared again until the following Ash Wednesday. It was only during the last century that this German (actually, ancient Roman) bread was adopted as an all-year tidbit, and its Lenten significance all but forgotten.

In Russia, the Lenten fare is the most meager of all European nations. Rigidly observed by the faithful far into the twentieth century, the traditional fast is still kept by old people: no meat, no fish, no milk (nor anything made of milk), no butter, no eggs, no sugar or candy. The diet during this period consists of bread made with water and salt, vegetables, raisins, honey, and raw fruit.

The Polish people's main staples in Lent include

herring (smoked or cooked), and *zur,* a mush made of fermented rye meal and water, which serves as a base for some Lenten soups. Here is the recipe of a typical Lenten soup (*Postna Zupa*) in Poland:

2 qts. cold water	1 onion
4 carrots	2 sprigs parsley
4 stalks celery	2 tbsp. butter
salt and pepper	

Wash vegetables, cut into small pieces and sauté in butter under cover until they turn yellow. Add water and simmer for half hour. Strain before serving.

Another popular Lenten soup is the *Postna Grochowka,* yellow split pea soup:

1 lb. yellow split peas	3 bay leaves
3 qts. water	4 whole allspice
¼ tsp. pepper	4 whole peppercorns
2 tsp. salt	1 cup diced carrots

Boil all ingredients except carrots slowly for about 4 hours or until peas are tender. Add carrots 2 hours before soup is done.

In the sixteenth century, when Erasmus Ciolek, the Bishop of Plock, brought the papal permission from Rome to eat meat on Wednesdays in Lent, no one was found in the whole kingdom of Poland who would use this privilege. However, under King

67

Sigismund August (1572) meat was served for the first time at the royal table because the German guests did not fast. This was the beginning of relaxation of the Lenten fast in Poland, especially in the cities.

Among the Ukrainians, neither meat nor dairy products are used by those who keep the strict fast. During Lent meals are never cooked, only vegetables, fruit, honey, and special bread are eaten.

Mourning · A character of mourning was always an important feature of the season of Lent. People would give up certain pleasures, entertainments, and festivities. Even within the liturgy this mourning was clearly expressed; no flowers decorated the altars, the organs went silent, weddings and other solemnities were banned, and the liturgical colors (purple and black) proclaimed the spirit of penance and grief. These laws are still followed in the Catholic Church, though somewhat mitigated from their original severity. In medieval times people would forgo all private entertainments at home that were of joyous and hilarious nature.

At the royal courts in past centuries, Lent was an official period of mourning. The monarchs and their households dressed in black, as did most of the nobility and people in general. England remained loyal to this custom even after the Reformation; Queen Elizabeth I (1603) and the ladies of her court wore black all through Lent. In Russia, up to the twentieth century, all secular music ceased in Lent. During the first and last weeks all public amusements were forbidden. Women dressed in black and laid their ornaments aside. In the rural sections of Poland, dancing and singing still cease on Ash Wednesday. Both men and women don clothes of dark and somber color; the girls relinquish their finery and multicolored ribbons, and an atmosphere of devout recollection descends over the entire village. In many countries the expressions of mourning are now restricted to the last days of Holy Week, as in the Latin nations where women dress in black on Good Friday. In Malta, the men, too, wear black.

Confession · The Church imposes on its members the duty of receiving the sacraments of Penance and Holy Communion at least once a year, during Lent or Easter time. Though most of the faithful approach the sacraments oftener, the "Easter confession" is still singled out in various countries as a solemn rite. It is usually made in Lent, and the Church provides special services of preparation such as annual missions for the congregations. These services are very

69

popular in the Latin countries. They are called *misiones* in the Spanish-speaking parts, *esercizi* (spiritual exercises) in Italy, *retraites* (retreats) in France and Canada. The original purpose of the Lenten missions was to help people prepare for a good confession.

In Russia, the faithful kept a specially strict fast during the whole week preceding their Easter confession. Starting on Monday, they attended two services a day. On Saturday, before going to confession, they would bow deeply to each member of their household, including the servants, and utter the age-old phrase, "In the name of Christ, forgive me if I have offended you." The answer was, "God will forgive you." Thus prepared, they made their confession on Saturday, and went to Communion on Sunday. Coming home from Mass and Communion, they again faced their whole family; but this time everyone embraced them with smiles and congratulations, flowers decorated the room and the breakfast table, and the entire household shared in the joy of the one who had received his Easter Communion. Similar traditions are still observed among the other Slavic nations. It was a custom in Austria for men and boys coming home from their Easter confession to decorate their hats with flowers and distribute pretzels to all in the house while receiving congratulations and good wishes.

Laetare Sunday · The fourth Sunday in Lent (Mid-Lent) derives its Latin name from the first word of the Mass text, *"Laetare Jerusalem"* (Rejoice, o Jerusalem). It is a day of joy within the mourning season. The altars may be decorated with flowers, organ playing is permitted, and the priests may wear rose-colored vestments instead of purple. The reason for such display of joy is explained in a sermon by Pope Innocent III (1216):

On this Sunday, which marks the middle of Lent, a measure of consoling relaxation is provided, so that the faithful may not break down under the severe strain of Lenten fast but may continue to bear the restrictions with a refreshed and easier heart.[31]

As a symbol of this joy the popes used to carry a golden rose in their right hand when returning from the celebration of Mass. Pope Leo IX (1051) calls this custom an "ancient institution." Originally it was a single rose of natural size, but since the fifteenth century it has consisted of a cluster or branch of roses wrought of pure gold and set with precious stones in brilliant workmanship by famous artists. The popes bless it every year, and often they

71

confer it upon churches, shrines, cities, or distinguished persons as a token of esteem and paternal affection. In case of such a bestowal, a new rose is made during the subsequent year.

The meaning and symbolism of the golden rose is expressed in the prayer of blessing. It represents Christ in the shining splendor of His majesty, the "flower sprung from the root of Jesse." From this ecclesiastical custom Laetare Sunday acquired its German name, *Rosensonntag* (Sunday of the Rose).

In this country Laetare Sunday receives much publicity in the papers because of Notre Dame's bestowal each year (since 1883) of the Laetare Medal on an American lay Catholic distinguished in literature, art, science, philanthropy, sociology, or other field of achievement. It is an adaptation of the papal custom of the golden rose, and the medal is made of heavy gold and black enamel tracings bearing the inscription *"Magna est veritas et praevalebit"* (Truth is mighty and shall prevail). It is suspended from a bar on which is lettered "Laetare Medal."

In England a charming tradition developed toward the end of the Middle Ages. On Laetare or Mid-Lent Sunday, boys and girls who lived away from home (as apprentices, servants, etc.) were given permission to go home to visit their mother church, in which they were baptized or had been brought up.

72

They always carried with them gifts to put on the altar. The original reason for this was because the first words of the Mass, "*Laetare Jerusalem,*" were considered in medieval times to be addressed to the "second Jerusalem" (the Church). And as the Jews called Jerusalem "Mother Jerusalem," so the Christians later called the church which gave them spiritual birth in baptism, "Mother Church." It was also the custom for the boys and girls to visit their own mother on the same day. They brought her flowers and simnel cakes (a rich plum cake; from *simila,* fine flour) and would do all the housework for her. This old custom still survives in certain parts of England, and the cakes are sold in London as well as provincial towns. Hence the name "Mothering Sunday" and the famous old saying, "He who goes a-mothering finds violets in the lane." An ancient carol entitled "Mothering Sunday" (It Is the Day of All the Year) may be found in the *Oxford Book of Carols.*[32] The tune is taken from an old German song of the fourteenth century. Robert Herrick (1674) mentioned the custom in his poem *To Dianeme:*

> I'll to thee a simnel bring
> 'Gainst thou go'st a-mothering,
> So that when she blesseth thee,
> Half that blessing thou'lt give me.

73

Our own Mother's Day, first celebrated in May 1914, does not have either the same origin or historical background, but the central idea of bestowing special favors and little gifts on our mothers in appreciation and love is similar. In many churches sermons are devoted on that day to the greatest mother of all, the Blessed Mother, Mary.

Mid-Lent · The week from the Wednesday before to the Wednesday after Laetare is called "Mid-Lent" in most countries. It is a time of many popular customs and traditions, most of them connected with ancient spring lore. In Germany and among the northern Slavic nations the "burial of winter" is celebrated in rural sections. In Poland children carry the effigy of a stork through the village; thus they greet the return of the bird as a harbinger of the approaching summer. In France and Canada, Mid-Lent is kept with a joyous meal and entertainment in the home. A rite performed in central and southern Europe is the decoration of wells and fountains with branches and flowers, to celebrate their final liberation from winter's ice. Laetare Sunday is called *Fontana* (Sunday of Fountains) in parts of Italy and France because of this.

In Germany, Austria, and among the Western Slavs, Laetare Sunday used to be the day of announcing the engagements of young people (*Lieb-statt Sonntag; Druzebna*). In Bohemia the boys would send messengers to the homes of their girl friends to deliver the solemn proposal. In Austria the girls of the village lined up in front of the church after Mass; their boy friends would take them by the hand and lead them back into the house of God, and thus "propose" to them by a silent act of religious import. After having prayed together, the couple would seal their engagement with a special meal. It is a curious fact that these engagement customs were called "Valentine," although they did not take place on Saint Valentine's day. The name is explained by the fact that Saint Valentine was the heavenly patron of young lovers and engaged couples.

In Ireland not only Mid-Lent but the whole season of Lent is the traditional time of matchmaking (*cleamhnas*). The older people visit each other's homes to discuss the possibilities of matching their sons and daughters. Among the young generation, there is much fun poked at those not yet married. In olden times the roisterers (practical jokers) would try to tie a rope around unmarried men and girls in the days before Lent, and "drag them off to the Skellig," a place associated with wedding rites in ancient times. In some parts of Ireland weddings

75

are held only on Easter Sunday, after the last preparations have been made during Lent.

Wednesday of the fourth week in Lent is called
"Middle Cross Day" in the Greek Church (Russians,
Ukrainians, Serbs, Greeks, etc.); it is a tradition to
bake little cakes shaped in the form of a cross, which
have to be eaten on this day.

Lenten Hymns · Most of the medieval Lenten songs
are translations or adaptations of Latin hymns used
in the Divine Office. The poem of Saint Gregory the
Great (604), *Audi benige conditor* (Kind Maker of
the World, O Hear), is recited during Vespers in
Lent. It inspired many popular Lenten songs during
the Middle Ages. In the English language alone,
more than twenty translations are known.

Another hymn ascribed to Saint Gregory is *Clarum
decus jejunii* (The Sacred Time of Lenten Fast).
An English translation, with a melody by Johann
Sebastian Bach (1750) may be found in the Protes-
tant Episcopal hymnal.[88] Other Latin hymns include
Ex more docti mystico (By Mystical Tradition
Taught), which is recited daily at the Office of the
Matins; its authorship is also ascribed to Saint
Gregory. *O sol salutis* (O Jesus, Saving Sun of
Grace), by an unknown author of the seventh or
eighth century, is used at the Lauds during Lent.

76

A favorite modern Lenten hymn is the poem by Claudia F. Hernaman (1898), "Lord, who throughout these forty days for us didst fast and pray . . . ," which was first published in her *Child's Book of Praise* in England, 1873.

Lenten Devotions · The prevailing popular devotion in Lent is, quite naturally, the veneration of the suffering Lord and the meditation on His Passion and death. Both the Eastern and Western Churches practice the touching devotion of the fourteen Stations of the Cross, which originated in the time of the Crusades, when the knights and pilgrims began to follow in prayerful meditation the route of Christ's way to Calvary. This devotion spread in Europe and developed into its present form through the zealous efforts of the Franciscan friars in the fourteenth and fifteenth centuries. As custodians of the shrines in the Holy Land, the Franciscans are still entrusted with the official erection and blessing of new Stations.

The Polish people have a deeply devotional Lenten service called *Gorzkie Zale* (Bitter Sorrows), a series of prayers, hymns, and meditations. It was first published in its present form in 1707, and no book in the Polish language was ever published in more editions. The Fathers of the Congregation of Missions (Lazarists) helped to spread this devotion throughout the whole nation. Immigrants brought it to America, where it is equally beloved and treasured among people of Polish descent. The tunes and words are uncommonly moving in their plaintive simplicity. Here are a few stanzas of the introductory hymn, in English translation with the ancient tune. (The second line of every stanza is repeated when sung.)

Bitter sorrows, deep and renting,
Pierce our hearts in great lamenting.

Fill our eyes with tears of anguish,
Make our souls in pity languish,

As the Savior's death we ponder
With compassion, grief and wonder:

Touch our hearts, O Christ, most holy,
With compunction, strong and lowly.

Through thy passion, borne in meekness
Free us, Lord, from sin and weakness.

Following thy painful paces,
May we share thy passion's graces.

CHAPTER 7

Passiontide

The fifth Sunday in Lent, called "Passion Sunday," occurs two weeks before Easter and inaugurates Passiontide, the final and particularly solemn preparations for the great feast. As a liturgical season, Passiontide is older than Lent, having been established by the Church as a period of fasting as early as the third century. During the first four weeks of Lent the spirit of personal penance prevailed, but these last fourteen days were devoted entirely to the meditation of Christ's Passion. Among the Slavic nations Passion Sunday is also called "Silent Sunday" and "Quiet Sunday."

On the eve of Passion Sunday the crucifixes, statues, and pictures in the churches are draped in purple cloth as a sign of mourning. This custom originated in Rome, where in ancient times the images of the papal chapel in the Vatican used to be shrouded when the deacon sang the concluding words of the Sunday Gospel, "Jesus hid himself and went out of the temple" (John 8, 59). The liturgical services of Passiontide are based on what happened to our Lord during the last days before His death, leading up to the mysteries of the Passion. (Mystery, in this connection, is the religious term for any episode of Christ's life related in the Gospels.) The Mass texts are dominated by the thought of the Just One, persecuted by His enemies, as He approaches the supreme sacrifice on Golgotha.

Feast of the Seven Sorrows · On Friday after Passion Sunday the Church celebrates the Feast of the Seven Sorrows of the Blessed Virgin, commemorating events of pain and suffering in her life, as recorded in the Gospels. The devotion to the sufferings of Mary was very popular and widely practiced in medieval times. In 1423, a synod at Cologne introduced a Mass text and prescribed a feast in honor of the Seven Sorrows to be annually held in Western

Germany. In 1727, Pope Benedict XIII (1730) extended this feast to the whole Church.

As sequence (hymn after the Gradual of the Mass) the Church employs the famous Latin poem *Stabat Mater Dolorosa* which originally was written as a prayer for private devotion by an unknown author (probably a Franciscan) in the thirteenth century. It is often attributed to the Franciscan Jacobus de Benedictis (1306), better known under his popular name Jacopone da Todi. His authorship, however, is still not certain.

The Stabat Mater has been translated from the Latin into the vernacular among all Christian nations, and is a greatly cherished Lenten hymn everywhere. First published in England in 1748, numerous English translations have appeared. The familiar tune was taken from a German hymn book (1661) of the Diocese of Mainz.

Stabat Mater Dolorosa
Juxta crucem lacrymosa

81

Dum pendebat filius
Cujus animam gementem
Contristatam et dolentem
Pertransivit gladius.

By the cross the Mother-maiden
Weeping stood and sorrow-laden,
   While her Jesus hung above;
Through her heart, in anguish heaving,
With a mother's sorrow grieving,
   Ran the sword of suffering love.

There are several outstanding compositions of the Stabat Mater in its original Latin text. The best one is generally acknowledged to be that of Pierluigi Palestrina (1594), a masterpiece in choral music. The style employed in the opening of the work is strikingly effective, and similar music since then has been described as being in the "Palestrina Stabat Mater" style.

The Stabat Mater of Gioacchino Rossini (1868) is also well known, a cantata somewhat operatic in manner; the solo *Cuius Animam* has been a favorite showpiece of tenors for many years. The Stabat Mater of Antonin Dvořák, first presented to the general public at London in 1884, is a much more substantial composition than Rossini's.

In Latin countries, especially in Spain and South America, the Feast of the Seven Sorrows is a great day of popular devotions. Thousands throng every church to visit the shrine of the Sorrowful Mother, which is radiant with many lights and richly decorated with flowers, palms, and shade-grown clusters of pale young wheat. In central Europe, where the feast is called "Friday of Sorrows" (*Schmerzensfreitag*), popular devotions are held, and for dinner a soup is served consisting of seven bitter herbs (*Siebenkräutersuppe*): *Brunnkress* (watercress); *Petersilie* (parsley); *Lauch* (leek or chives); *Nessel* (nettle); *Sauerklee* (sour clover); *Schlüsselblume* (primrose or yellow cowslip); and *Spinat* (spinach).

Holy Week · In the Greek Church the last week of Lent bears the solemn title "The Sacred and Great Week" (*He hagia kai megale hebdomas*). In the Latin Church the official term is "The Greater Week" (*hebdomada major*). The popular names are "Great Week" among the Slavic nations, and "Holy Week" in other countries. The German name *Karwoche* means "Week of Mourning." In ancient times Holy Week was also called "Week of Remission," since the public sinners were absolved on Maundy Thursday. Another name was "Laborious Week" (*semaine peineuse*) because of the increased burden of penance and fasting. The faithful of the Eastern Churches also call it the "Week of Salvation."

83

From the very beginning of Christianity this week has always been devoted to a special commemoration of Christ's Passion and death through the practice of meditation, prayer, fasting, and penance. After the great persecutions, the Christian emperors both of the Eastern and Western Roman Empires issued various decrees forbidding not only amusements and games, but also regular work in trade, business, professions, and courts. The sacred days were to be spent free from worldly occupations, entirely devoted to religious exercises. Every year during Holy Week an imperial edict granted pardon to a majority of those detained in prison; in the courts many charges were withdrawn in honor of Christ's Passion.[34]

Following this custom, kings and rulers in medieval days retired from all secular business during Holy Week to spend the time in recollection and prayer, often within the seclusion of a monastery. Farmers set aside their plows, artisans their tools, schools and government offices closed, and courts did not sit. Popular feeling caused the banning not only of music, dancing, and secular singing but also of hunting and any other kind of sport. It was truly a "quiet" and "holy" week even in public life.

Spring Cleaning · According to an ancient tradition, the three days after Palm Sunday are devoted in many countries to a thorough cleaning of the house, the most vigorous of the whole year. Carpets, couches, arm chairs, and mattresses are carried into the open and every speck of dust beaten out of them. Women scrub and wax floors and furniture, change curtains, wash windows; the home is buzzing with activity. No time is wasted on the usual kitchen work, the meals are very casual and light. On Wednesday night everything has to be back in place, glossy and shining, ready for the great feast. In Poland and other Slavic countries people also decorate their homes with green plants and artificial flowers made of colored paper carrying out ancient and really enchanting designs.

This traditional spring cleaning, of course, is to make the home as neat as possible for the greatest holidays of the year, a custom taken over from the ancient Jewish practice of a ritual cleansing and sweeping of the whole house as prescribed in preparation for the Feast of Passover.

Passion Hymns · The most important hymns in honor of the Redeemer's Passion are used in the liturgical office of Passiontide. From early centuries translations of these hymns have also served as popular Lenten songs. At the Matins, in Passiontide, the Church intones the famous song *Pangue lingua gloriosi lauream certaminis,* written by Venantius Fortunatus (602), Bishop of Poitiers. This is frequently sung in choral groups all over the world. Here is the first stanza of an English translation by John M. Neale (1851):

> Sing, my tongue, the glorious battle,
> Sing the winning of the fray;
> Now above the cross, the trophy,
> Sound the high triumphant lay:
> Tell how Christ, the world's Redeemer
> As a victim won the day.

At Vespers, in Passiontide, another hymn by Venantius Fortunatus is heard. He composed it in 569, when the relics of the true Cross, sent by Emperor Justinian II of East Rome, arrived at the monastery of Poitiers: *Vexilla Regis prodeunt* (The Royal Banners Forward Go). Of this hymn, about fifty English translations since the fourteenth century are known.

A favorite Passion hymn is the poem by Peter Abelard (1142), *Solus ad victimam procedis, Domine:*

Alone, o Lord, thou goest to the slaughter
To die, so that we may be saved and live.
What can we sinners say, how can we thank thee?
Thy loving death, o Lord, may all our sins forgive.

An old English text of this hymn was sung in America to a tune called *Bangor*. There is a charming New England legend which relates that the city of Bangor, Maine, received its name because the minister of the town absent-mindedly gave the name of this tune, which he was humming, to the clerk who filled out the papers of incorporation.

An old German song, *O Haupt voll Blut und Wunden,* written by Paul Gerhardt in 1656, was often translated into English; it is sung both in Catholic and Protestant churches during Lent. The tune is taken from an old German folk song composed by Hans L. Hassler, and published in 1601. Johann Sebastian Bach employs this melody repeatedly in his *Saint Matthew Passion.*

O blessed Head so wounded,
Reviled and put to scorn!

87

> O sacred Head, disfigured
> And crowned with piercing thorn!
>
> O Head, what precious jewels
> Should crown thee, rich and bright;
> In tears I will adore thee
> And tremble at thy sight.

Of modern Passion hymns, the most famous is the American Negro spiritual "Were You There When They Crucified My Lord?" It was first published in 1899, and has since become a favorite song in many churches. The traditional melody was arranged by the Reverend Charles Winfred Douglas (1944), and made famous by the Negro tenor, Roland Hayes.

There are numberless ancient English poems written in honor of Christ's Passion which at one time probably served as church hymns but are forgotten today. As an example here is one stanza of the poem *Filius Regis mortuus est* (Dead Is the Son of Heaven's King), written by an unknown author of the Middle English period; it pictures the sorrowful complaints of Mary over the death of her Son:

> Ye creatures cruel, Iron, Steel, sharp Thorn,
> How dare ye thus your best Friend slay?
> The Holiest Child that e'er was born
> Did wounds and torment on Him lay!

With spear and nails His Flesh have torn:
Spear! the smith's hand why didst not stay.
That ground thy blade so sharp this morn,
That to His heart didst cleave a way?
I cry on thee both night and day,
A maiden's Son to death didst wrest,
Forlorn, I wring my hands alway,
Filius Regis mortuus est!

Americans of all denominations are familiar with the famous Passion Play at Oberammergau, a beautiful little village standing in a lonely valley almost on the watershed of the Bavarian Alps. During its many tableaux there is scarcely a face among the thousands of spectators that is not wet with tears at the sight of these masterful and deeply touching representations of Christ's suffering and death. Similar plays are performed on a more moderate scale in many places both in Europe and America.

CHAPTER 8

Palm Sunday

As soon as the Church obtained her freedom in the fourth century, the faithful in Jerusalem re-enacted the solemn entry of Christ into their city on the Sunday before Easter, holding a procession in which they carried branches and sang the "Hosanna" (Matthew 21, 1-11). In the early Latin Church, people attending Mass on this Sunday would hold aloft twigs of olives, which were not, however, blessed in those days.

This "Palm Sunday" procession, and the blessing of "palms," seems to have originated in the Frankish Kingdom. The earliest mention of these ceremonies is found in the *Sacramentary* of the Abbey of Bobbio

in northern Italy (beginning of the eighth century).
The rite was soon accepted in Rome and incorporated into the liturgy. The prayers used today are
of Roman origin. A Mass was celebrated in some
church outside the walls of Rome, and there the
palms were blessed. Then a solemn procession moved
into the city to the basilica of the Lateran or to Saint
Peter's, where the Pope sang a second Mass. The first
Mass, however, was soon discontinued, and in its
place only the ceremony of blessing was performed.
Even today the ritual of the blessing clearly follows
the structure of a Mass up to the Sanctus.

Everywhere in medieval times, following the
Roman custom, a procession composed of the clergy
and laity carrying palms moved from a chapel or
shrine outside the town, where the palms were
blessed, to the cathedral or main church. Our Lord
was represented in the procession, either by the
Blessed Sacrament or by a crucifix, adorned with
flowers, carried by the celebrant of the Mass. Later,
in the Middle Ages, a quaint custom arose of drawing a wooden statue of Christ sitting on a donkey
(the whole image on wheels) in the center of the
procession. These statues (Palm Donkey; *Palmesel*)
are still seen in museums of many European cities.

As the procession approached the city gate, a boys'
choir stationed high above the doorway would greet

the Lord with the Latin song, *Gloria, laus et honor.* This hymn, which is still used today in the liturgy of Palm Sunday, was written by the Benedictine Theodulph, Bishop of Orleans (821):

> Glory, praise and honor,
> O Christ, our Savior-King,
> To thee in glad Hosannas
> Inspired children sing.

After this song, there followed a dramatic salutation before the Blessed Sacrament or the image of Christ. Both clergy and laity knelt and bowed in prayer, arising to spread cloths and carpets on the ground, throwing flowers and branches in the path of the procession. The bells of the churches pealed, and the crowds sang the "Hosanna" as the colorful procession entered the cathedral for the solemn Mass.

In medieval times this dramatic celebration was restricted more and more to a procession around the church. The crucifix in the church yard was festively decorated with flowers. There the procession came to a halt. While the clergy sang the hymns and antiphons, the congregation dispersed among the tombs, each family kneeling at the grave of relatives. The celebrant sprinkled holy water over the graveyard, the procession formed again and entered the church. In France and England they still retain the custom of decorating graves and visiting the cemeteries on Palm Sunday.

The inspiring rites and ceremonies of ancient times have long since disappeared, only the sacred texts of the liturgy are still preserved. Today the blessing of palms and the procession (if any) are performed within the churches preceding the Mass. In America, Catholic, and some Episcopal, churches distribute palms to all the congregation.

The various names for the Sunday before Easter come from the plants used—palms (Palm Sunday) or branches in general (Branch Sunday; *Domingo de Ramos; Dimanche des Rameaux*). In most countries of Europe real palms are unobtainable, so in their place people use many other plants: olive branches (in Italy), box, yew, spruce, willows, and pussy willows. In fact, some plants have come to be called "palms" because of this usage, as the yew in Ireland, the willow in England (palm-willow) and in Germany (*Palmkätzchen*). From the use of willow branches Palm Sunday was called "Willow Sunday" in parts of England and Poland, and in Lithuania *Verbu Sekmadienis* (Willow-twig Sunday). The Greek Church uses the names "Sunday of the Palm-carrying" and "Hosanna Sunday."

Centuries ago it was customary to bless not only branches but also various flowers of the season (the flowers are still mentioned in the antiphons after the prayer of blessing).[35] Hence the name "Flower Sunday" which the day bore in many countries—"Flowering Sunday" or "Blossom Sunday" in England, *Blumensonntag* in Germany, *Pâsques Fleuris* in France, *Pascua Florida* in Spain, *Virágvasárnap* in Hungary, *Cvetna* among the Slavic nations, *Zaghkasart* in Armenia.

The term *Pascua Florida*, which in Spain originally meant just Palm Sunday, was later also applied to the whole festive season of Easter Week. Thus the State of Florida received its name when, on March 27, 1513 (Easter Sunday), Ponce de Leon first sighted the land and named it in honor of the great feast.

In central Europe, large clusters of such plants, interwoven with flowers and adorned with ribbons, are fastened to the top of a wooden stick. All sizes of such palm bouquets may be seen, from the small children's bush to rods of ten feet and more. The regular "palm," however, consists in most European countries of pussy willows bearing their catkin blossoms. In the Latin countries and in the United States, palm leaves are often shaped and woven into little crosses and other symbolic designs. This custom was originated by a suggestion in the ceremonial book for bishops, that "little crosses of palm" be attached

94

to the boughs wherever true palms are not available in sufficient quantity.[86]

In the ancient prayers for the blessing of the palms the Church uses these invocations:

May these branches of palms and olives be blessed, o Lord; and may we, through good works, meet Christ with palms and branches of olives, and through him enter into eternal joy.

O God, who didst bless the people that carried boughs to meet Jesus: bless also these branches of palms and olives which thy servants accept in faith and for the honor of thy name, that into whatever place they may be brought, the inhabitants of that place may obtain thy benediction, and thy right hand may preserve them from all adversity, whom thy Son, Jesus Christ our Lord, has redeemed.[37]

In the spirit of this blessing, the faithful reverently keep the palms in their homes throughout the year, usually attached to a crucifix or holy picture, or fastened on the wall. In South America they put the large palm bouquets behind the door. In Italy people offer blessed palms as a token of reconciliation and peace to those with whom they have quarreled or lived on unfriendly terms. The Ukrainians and Poles strike each other gently with the pussy-willow palms on Palm Sunday; this custom, called

Boze Rany (God's Wounds) they interpret as imitation of the scourging of our Lord, and they sing or recite the following ancient phrases:

> It is not I that strikes, it is the palm.
> Six nights hence—the great night!
> A week hence—the great day!

In Austria, Bavaria, and in the Slavic countries, farmers, accompanied by their families, walk through their fields and buildings on the afternoon of Palm Sunday. Praying and singing their ancient hymns, they place a sprig of blessed palms, in each lot of pasture or plowland, in every barn and stable, to avert the punishment of weather tragedies or diseases, and to draw God's blessing on the year's harvest and all their possessions.

The significant music of Palm Sunday is the chanting of the Passion. The word "Passion" in this connection means those passages of the Gospels which report the events of Christ's suffering and death, from the Last Supper to His burial. The Passions of all four Gospels are read or chanted in all Catholic churches during the liturgical services on certain days of Holy Week, and observed in varying degrees in many Protestant churches. On Palm Sunday, the Passion of Saint Matthew (26, 1—27, 66) is solemnly sung during Mass, in place of the usual Gospel.

The ancient liturgical rules prescribe that three clergymen of deacon's rank, vested in alb and stole, chant the sacred text. They are to alternate in contrasting voices. One (tenor) represents the Evangelist narrator; the second (high tenor) chants the voices of individuals and crowds; the third (bass) sings only the words of Christ.

The melodies prescribed for the liturgical chanting of the Passion are among the most impressive examples of Gregorian chant, and for many centuries remained the only Passion music, until the non-liturgical works on the Passion were written.

The Gregorian melody to which the Latin text *Hosanna Filio David* (Hosanna to the Son of David) is sung has been used by many composers for Palm Sunday music because of its triumphant and joyous expression, and it is heard in both Catholic and Protestant churches. Both Palestrina and Thomas Luis Victoria (1613) have utilized this liturgical chant. The text has been translated into the vernacular and sung by the faithful to various melodies.

Les Rameaux (The Palms), by Jean B. Faure (1914), is perhaps the best known of musical works for Palm Sunday. The composer was a greatly admired operatic baritone who wrote a few vocal pieces. "The Palms," however, is the only composition which survived him. In recent years its popularity has waned somewhat, but it is still heard in many churches. An older generation could hardly imagine a Palm Sunday service without "The Palms."

CHAPTER 9

Maundy Thursday

The solemn services of the sacred Triduum, the three days before Easter, begin on the preceding Wednesday evening with the public chanting of Tenebrae. This word means "darkness," since the candles in the sanctuary are extinguished one after another, until only one candle (representing Christ) remains and is carried behind the altar at the end of the ceremonies.

The Tenebrae service is the chanting of the Matins and Lauds, which are the first part of the daily Divine Office recited from the early centuries of Christianity. While on other days only the cathedral

99

chapters and many religious chant them in choir, on the Triduum of Holy Week they are performed in all principal churches, so that the congregations, too, may attend. Besides the psalms and antiphons, nine lessons (readings) are recited in the Matins. The first three lessons consist of quotations from the book of Lamentations of Jeremias, the second three of excerpts from the sermons of Saint Augustine, the final three of passages from the letters of Saint Paul. The Lauds, consisting of psalms, antiphons, and the hymn *Benedictus* (Luke 1, 68-79), close with the famous penitential prayer *Miserere* (Psalm 50).

The *Miserere* is often sung by a choir at the Tenebrae services. The most famous music for this psalm is the composition by Gregorio Allegri (sixteenth century). It consists of a double chorus for eight voices, was written for the papal choir during Holy Week, and was kept unpublished by order of the popes to reserve this music for exclusive use in the Sistine Chapel. So it remained until 1769, when Leopold Mozart brought his fourteen-year-old son, Wolfgang Amadeus Mozart, from Austria to Rome to hear the music of the Holy Week services in the papal chapel. The youthful genius was so thrilled with the Allegri *Miserere* that on returning to his lodgings he wrote out the entire eight-part chorus

100

from memory. The following day father and son returned to the Tenebrae service carrying the boy's manuscript, in order to check what he had written from memory. Only a few notes of the music needed correction. This prodigious feat was brought to the attention of the reigning pope, Clement XIV, who sent for father and son. The Mozarts feared that the Pope would be indignant at the plagiarism implied in the boy's act, but His Holiness praised him highly, and forthwith ordered the publication of the *Miserere* for the whole world to enjoy. Since then, throughout the Christian world, to hear this great masterpiece sung is one of the most moving experiences of Holy Week.

Every year during these services in the Sistine Chapel the papal choir performs the "Lamentations" by Palestrina, one of the most majestic pieces of sacred music ever written. Another choral piece by Palestrina is the beautiful *Improperia* (Reproaches), first heard in 1560, a work of great tenderness and solemnity. There are other musical compositions inspired by the "Reproaches," notably that of Victoria, the great rival of Palestrina.

The triangular candlestick used at Tenebrae, bearing fifteen candles, is called a hearse. The word comes from the Old English "herice," meaning har-

101

row, apparently suggested by the spikes upon which the candles were fixed. (The use of "hearse" for a vehicle carrying a coffin came also from the spiked structure for candles around a coffin.)

Another interesting feature of Tenebrae is the noise made at the conclusion of the rite. Like the whole service, this custom is quite ancient. It has been incorporated into the official instructions of the Roman Breviary, which prescribe that "some banging noise" be made when the prayers are finished.[88] Usually a wooden clapper is used, or the priests bang the seats of the pews with their Breviary books. This significant tradition has been explained from medieval times as indicating the confusion of Nature at the death of Christ (Matthew 27, 51). Actually its origin is the ancient monastic practice at the end of the choir service of the abbot giving the signal to move out of the pews by knocking the bench or sounding a clapper.

In the later Middle Ages very often the whole congregation took part in producing the noise. Boys would hit the pews with rods and sticks, people would cry out and stamp the ground with their feet. In Spain they even fired guns outside the church. In Germany and Austria the whole service was called *Pumpermette* (Noisy Matins). These excesses, however, have been suppressed long since, and the "noise" now is subdued and in the spirit of the occasion.

There are few services in the whole range of ancient Christian ritual more impressive than the office of Tenebrae. Desolation, anguish, and devotion are manifested in these prayers and ceremonies during the three days' dirge over the crucified Redeemer, as the Church cries out through the mouth of her priests and people, "Mine eyes are blinded with tears because the Comforter that should relieve me is far from me. Behold, all nations, if there be any sorrow like my sorrow." [89]

The second day of the celebration of Tenebrae bears the liturgical name "Thursday of the Lord's Supper" (*Feria Quinta in Coena Domini*). Of its many popular names the more generally known are:

Maundy Thursday (*le mandé;* Thursday of the *Mandatum*). The word *Mandatum* means "commandment." This name is taken from the first words sung at the ceremony of the washing of the feet, "A new commandment I give you" (John 13, 34); also from the commandment of Christ that we should imitate His loving humility in the washing of the feet (John 13, 14-17). Thus the term *Mandatum* (maundy) was applied to the rite of the feet-washing on this day.

103

Green Thursday. In all German-speaking countries people call Maundy Thursday by this name (*Gründonnerstag*). From Germany the term was adopted by the Slavic nations (*zeleny ctvrtek*) and in Hungary (*zöld csütörtök*). Scholars explain its origin from the old German word *grunen* (to mourn) which was later corrupted into *grün* (green). Another explanation is that in many places, before the thirteenth century, green vestments were used for the Mass that day.

Pure or *Clean Thursday.* This name emphasizes the ancient tradition that on Holy Thursday not only the souls were cleansed through the absolution of public sinners but the faithful in all countries also made it a great cleansing day of the body (washing, bathing, shaving, etc.) in preparation for Easter. Saint Augustine (430) mentioned this custom.[40] The Old English name was "Shere Thursday" (meaning sheer, clean), and the Scandinavian, *Skaer torsdag.* (Because of the exertions and thoroughness of this cleansing in an age when bathing was not an everyday affair, the faithful were exempted from fasting on Maundy Thursday.)

Holy or *Great Thursday.* The meaning of this title is obvious since it is the one Thursday of the year on which the sacred events of Christ's Passion are celebrated. The English-speaking nations and the people of the Latin countries use the term "Holy," while the Slavic populations generally apply the title "Great." The Ukrainians call it also the "Thursday of the Passion." In the Greek

104

Church it is called "The Holy and Great Thursday of the Mystic Supper."

In the early Christian centuries three Masses used to be celebrated on Maundy Thursday. The first (Mass of Remission) for the reconciliation of public sinners; the second (Mass of the Chrism) for the blessing of holy oils; the third (Mass of the Lord's Supper) in commemoration of the Last Supper of Christ and the institution of the Eucharist. This third Mass was celebrated in the evening, and in it the priests and people received Holy Communion. It is interesting to note that in medieval times Holy Thursday was the only day of the year when the faithful could receive the Blessed Sacrament at night after having taken their customary meals during the day (since it was not a fast day). Gradually the three Masses were replaced by one single Mass, which is still celebrated in our churches today. It is one of the most solemn and impressive Masses of the year, since the very "birthday" of the Holy Sacrifice is commemorated in it.

The altar is decorated, crucifix and tabernacle are veiled in white, and the priests wear rich vestments of white, the liturgical color of joy. At the beginning of the Mass the organ accompanies the choir, and through the Gloria a jubilant ringing of bells pro-

105

claims the festive memory of the institution of the Blessed Sacrament. After the Gloria the bells fall silent and are replaced by a wooden clapper and not heard again till the Gloria of the Easter Vigil is intoned on Holy Saturday.

Only one priest celebrates Mass in each church on Holy Thursday; the other priests and the lay people receive Communion from his hand, thus representing more vividly the scene of our Lord's Last Supper.

After the Mass, the Blessed Sacrament is carried in solemn procession, preceded by children strewing rose petals in its path. On a side altar, richly decorated with candles and flowers, the Blessed Sacrament is kept in the tabernacle until Good Friday morning. This "repository" altar is a highly venerated shrine in every church, visited by thousands of people. A popular custom in cities is to visit seven such shrines that day. Throughout the night, in many countries, groups of the clergy and laymen keep prayerful watch in honor of the agony of Christ.

In the Latin countries of Europe and South America the Maundy Thursday shrine is called *monumento*. It is much more elaborate than the shrines of other nations. Usually a special scaffolding with many steps, representing a sacred hill, is erected, so high that it almost reaches to the ceiling. On the top of this the Sacrament is elevated, raised above a glorious forest of candles, palms, orchids, lilies, and other decorations. Dressed in black, the city people visit at least seven such *monumentos,* which, in many places, are open through the night. On their way from church to church they say the Rosary.

After the Mass and the procession on Holy Thursday morning, the altars are "denuded" in a ceremony of deep significance. Priests robed in purple vestments remove the altar linen, decorations, candles, and veils from every altar and tabernacle except the repository shrine. Robbed of their vesture, the bare altars now represent the body of Christ, who was stripped of His garments. In medieval times the altars used to be washed with blessed water and wine, the priests using bundles of birch twigs or palms to cleanse and dry them. In the Vatican this ceremony is still performed by the canons of Saint Peter's after Tenebrae on Holy Thursday.

An ancient rite of Maundy Thursday now totally extinct was the solemn reconciliation of public penitents. As on Ash Wednesday, they again approached the church, dressed in sackcloth, barefoot, unshaven, weak, and feeble from their forty days' fast and penance. The bishop led them into the house of God, where after many prayers and exhortations he absolved them from their sins and crimes. With his

107

blessing, and an indulgence granted, they joyfully hurried home to bathe, shave, and cut their hair in preparation for Easter, and to resume their normal dress and routine of daily life which had been so harshly interrupted during the time of their public penance.

Finally, there is the ancient rite of the *Mandatum,* the washing of the feet. It is prescribed by the rules of the Roman Missal as follows:

After the altars are denuded, the clergy shall meet at a convenient hour for the Mandatum. The Gospel *Ante diem festum* (John 13, 1-17) is sung by the Deacon. After the Gospel the prelate puts off his cope and, fastening a towel around him, he kneels before each one of those who are chosen for the ceremony, washes, wipes and kisses the right foot.

From ancient times, all religious superiors, bishops, abbots, and prelates, performed the Maundy; so did the popes at all times. As early as 694 the Synod of Toledo prescribed the rite. Religious superiors of monasteries washed the feet of those subject to them, while the popes and bishops performed the ceremony on a number of clergy or laymen (usually twelve). In medieval times, and in some countries up to the present century, Christian emperors, kings, and lords washed the feet of old and poor men whom they

108

afterwards served at a meal and provided with appropriate alms.

In England, the kings used to wash the feet of as many men as they themselves were years old. After the Reformation, Queen Elizabeth I still adhered to the pious tradition; she is reported to have used a silver bowl of water scented with perfume when she washed the feet of poor women on Maundy Thursday. Today, all that is left of this custom in England is a distribution of silver coins by royal officials to as many poor persons as the monarch is years old.

In the Latin countries the washing of feet is still kept in many parish churches, where the pastor performs it on twelve old men or twelve boys. In Mexico and other sections of South America the Last Supper is often re-enacted in church, with the priest presiding and twelve men or boys, dressed as apostles, speaking the dialogue as recorded in the Gospels. In Malta, a "Last Supper Table" is richly laden by the faithful with food that is later distributed to the poor.

The Greek Church celebrates a night vigil from Holy Thursday to Good Friday, in which the texts of the Passion, collected from the Bible and arranged in twelve chapters (called the "Twelve Gospels") are sung or read, with prayers, prostrations, and hymns after every chapter. In the Cathedral of Constantinople, the East Roman emperors used to attend this service; hence it was called the "Royal Hours." Its original name is *Pannuchida* (all-night service). In Russia people would carry home the candles that they had used in this vigil, and with them they would light the lamps that burned day and night before the family *ikons* (holy pictures). The Ukrainians celebrate the "Royal Hours" on Good Friday morning.

Many popular customs and traditions are connected with Maundy Thursday. There is, above all, the universal children's legend that the bells "fly to Rome" after the Gloria of the Mass. In Germany and central Europe the little ones are told that the church bells make a pilgrimage to the tomb of the apostles, or that they visit the Holy Father (Pope) to be blessed by him, then sleep on the roof of St. Peter's until Holy Saturday morning. In France the story is that the bells fly to Rome to fetch the Easter eggs that they will drop on their return into every house where the children are good and well behaved.

In some Latin countries sugared almonds are eaten by everybody on Maundy Thursday. From this custom it bears the name "Almond Day" in the Azores. In central Europe the name "Green Thursday" inspired a tradition of eating green things. The main meal starts with a soup of green herbs, followed

110

by a bowl of spinach with boiled or fried eggs, and meat with dishes of various green salads.

Following the ecclesiastical custom, the bells on farm buildings are silent in Germany and Austria, and dinner calls are made with wooden clappers. In rural sections of Austria boys with clappers go through the villages and towns, announcing the hours (since the church clock is stopped). These youngsters (*Ratschenbuben*) sing a different stanza each hour, in which they commemorate the events of Christ's Passion. Here is the traditional text of such a song, for nine o'clock at night on Holy Thursday:

> We beg you, people, hear and hark!
> It's nine o'clock, and fully dark.
> O, think of the pain which Christ has felt,
> When, praying for us, in the garden He knelt.
> > In agony fretting,
> > Blood and water sweating,
> He suffers in darkness who is our Light:
> Remember it, folks, at nine o'clock night!

CHAPTER 10

Good Friday

From the earliest centuries, Good Friday was universally celebrated in the Church as a day of sadness, mourning, fasting, and prayer. The *Apostolic Constitutions* (fourth century) called it a "day of mourning, not a day of festive joy." Saint Ambrosius (397), Archbishop of Milan, mentioned Good Friday as a "day of bitterness on which we fast." [41] Reverend Frederick Oakely (1880) expressed the mood of the Church in one of his poems:

> Thy heart, O widowed Spouse, is like to break;
>   Thou canst not speak,

Thou canst but hide thy face and sob and weep
In anguish deep.[42]

The liturgical title in the Western Church is "Friday of the Preparation" (*Feria sexta in Parasceve*). At the time of Christ, the Jews used the Greek word *Paraskeue* (getting ready) for Friday, meaning the day of preparation for the Sabbath. This word is now used both in the Oriental and Occidental Churches. Popular names are "Holy Friday" among the Latin nations, "Great Friday" among the Slavic peoples (*petok veliki*) and Hungarians (*nagypéntek*), "Friday of Mourning" in German (*Karfreitag*), "Long Friday" in Norway (*Langfredag*), and "Good Friday" in English and Dutch.

The early Church, following apostolic tradition, employed the hallowed term "Pasch" (from Hebrew *pesach*, passover) both to Good Friday and Easter Sunday. Thus Good Friday is called the "Pasch of Crucifixion" (*pascha staurosimon*), Easter the "Pasch of Resurrection" (*pascha anastasimon*), and the Eastern Church has kept these names up to our day.

The first part of the Good Friday service is the only example of an ancient Roman *Synaxis* (prayer meeting without Mass) that has survived to the present. It consists of a silent prostration before the altar,

113

followed by lessons (readings from the Bible), chanting of the Passion of Saint John, prayers, and the Great Litany for the necessities of the Church, the celebrant starting every invocation with the words, "*Oremus, dilectissimi nobis*" (Let us pray, dearest brethren).

After the *Synaxis* one of the most moving ceremonies of the year takes place, the Adoration of the Cross. (The word "adoration" in this instance is a translation of the Greek *proskunesis*, which meant a tribute of the highest honor, performed by a prostration to the ground.) In medieval England and Germany the ceremony was called "creeping to the Cross" (*zum Kreuz kriechen*).

The celebrating priest unveils the crucifix in three stages, singing, "Behold the wood of the Cross, on which hung the Salvation of the world"; to which the choir and people, kneeling and reverently bowing, answer, "Come, let us adore!" Then the crucifix is placed on a pillow in front of the altar. The priest and his assistants approach it, genuflecting three times, and devoutly kiss the feet of the image. The rest of the clergy and the lay people follow, performing the same humble act of veneration. Meanwhile the choir sings the ancient *Improperia* (complaints) of Christ:

My people, what have I done to thee?
Or in what have I grieved thee? Answer me!

I brought thee out of the land of Egypt:
And thou hast prepared a cross for thy Savior.

For thy sake I scourged Egypt and its first-born:
And thou didst scourge me and deliver me to death.

In answer the choir sings the invocation called *Trisagion* (thrice holy) in Latin and Greek:

O holy God,
O strong, holy One,
O holy, immortal One, have mercy on us.

The hymn *Crux Fidelis*, written by Venantius Fortunatus (602) follows this:

Faithful Cross, O throne of mercy,
Tree all noble and divine!
There's no tree on earth that carries
Fruit and flower such as thine:
Sweet and holy, nails and wood,
Sweet the burden, pure and good.

The Adoration of the Cross was adopted by the Roman Church from Jerusalem, where the true Cross of Christ was thus venerated every year on Good Friday as early as the fourth century. Egeria, a lady from the Roman province of Spain, made a pilgrim-

115

age to the Holy Land in A.D. 380, and has left us in her diary the first description of this ceremony. It is of special interest that, according to her report, not only the Cross but also the title board bearing the inscription (John 19, 19-22) was presented to the pilgrims. They were allowed to kiss, but not to touch, the sacred objects. When the Mohammedans conquered Jerusalem under Sultan Saladin, in 1187, they took the relics away, and no trace of them was ever found. Fortunately, a piece of the true Cross was brought to Rome in the fourth century, and from it many churches in all countries have received small particles as relics.

After the solemn veneration of the Cross, the Blessed Sacrament is carried in procession from the repository shrine (where it was placed the day before) to the main altar. Then the Mass of the Presanctified is celebrated. As the word "presanctified" indicates, this is not a real Mass, since the host was already consecrated on the previous day, Holy Thursday. It is only a solemn rite presenting ceremonies of the Mass, but not the Divine Sacrifice itself. On the day on which Christ offered Himself on the Cross for the redemption of the world, the Church reverently abstains from performing the same sacrifice in its unbloody repetition, which otherwise is offered

116

every day according to His command (1 Cor. 11, 23-26).

At the completion of the Mass of the Presanctified the official service of the liturgy is finished. The altar is stripped again, the tabernacle is left open, no lights burn in the sanctuary. Only the crucifix, now unveiled, takes the place of honor in front of the empty tabernacle.

The faithful, however, practice various additional devotions on Good Friday. In all countries such devotional exercises are now held with traditional piety.

The most ancient and impressive of these extraliturgical Good Friday rites is the shrine of the Holy Sepulcher, a custom that started over a thousand years ago and is still observed in many countries. In past centuries it was a universal tradition in England and France. The rite was performed with liturgical texts and ceremonies, although it was never officially incorporated in the Roman liturgy. In some countries a crucifix or the Blessed Sacrament (or both together) were borne in solemn procession to a shrine called the Sepulcher. There the priest deposited them in a sort of tabernacle shaped like a tomb chamber. The faithful visited the shrine all through Good Friday and Holy Saturday.[43]

An interesting record of this solemn service can

117

still be found in the records of the town of Durham, England:

Within the church of Durham upon Good Friday there was a marvellous solemn service in which service time after the Passion was sung, two of the eldest monks took a goodly large crucifix all of gold of the semblance of our Saviour Christ, nailed upon the Cross. . . . The service being ended the two monks carried the Cross to the Sepulchre with great reverence (which Sepulchre was set up that morning on the north side of the choir, nigh unto the High Altar, before the service time), and there did lay it within the said Sepulchre with great devotion.

Today, the custom of the Holy Sepulcher is still universally observed in central and eastern Europe and in the Latin countries. After the liturgical service, the priests carry the Blessed Sacrament in splendid procession to the side altar. The monstrance in which the Sacrament is borne is covered with a transparent veil of white lace to symbolize the burial shroud of Christ. A representation of the Lord's tomb, showing an image of the Savior resting in death, awaits the procession. This shrine is decorated with many candles, palms, flowers, and lights. There the Blessed Sacrament is exposed on a throne for the veneration of the faithful. All through Good Friday and Holy Saturday, people come in great numbers, kneel in devout prayer before the Eucharistic Lord, actually

118

a spiritual "wake" of devotion and adoration. In Austria it is a traditional custom that soldiers of the army in parade uniform, with steel helmets and fixed bayonets, man a guard of honor at the shrine, and thus atone for the irreverent guard of Roman soldiers at the tomb of Christ.

In Spanish-speaking countries of Europe and South America the *monumento* is taken down on Good Friday morning, and in its place a representation of Calvary is erected, with life-size figures of Christ on the Cross, the Blessed Mother, Saint John, and Mary Magdalen. At three o'clock in the afternoon, altar boys light up flashing powder to represent lightning and make a noise in imitation of thunder. Then the priest mounts a ladder to detach the body of Christ from the Cross. He takes it down and places it in the shrine of the Sepulcher. There the faithful visit and pray all through the evening. It is customary to recite thirty-three credos in honor of the years of our Lord's life.

In the United States shrines of the Holy Sepulcher may be seen in many national churches of Catholics from central and eastern Europe and from the Latin countries.

A similar solemnity is observed in the Greek Church. On the afternoon of Good Friday, the elders of the parish carry a cloth containing a picture of our

119

Lord's body resting in death. Followed by the priest, they walk in procession to the shrine of the Sepulcher, where the cloth is placed on a table to be venerated by the people. The entire ceremony and the shrine are called *Platsenitsia* (winding sheet) among the Ukrainians and other Slavs of the Oriental Church.

In Russia a silver coffin bearing a cross was placed in the center of the church and surrounded with lights and flowers. One after another the faithful, creeping on their knees, approached to kiss the cross and to venerate the image of Christ's body painted on the "winding sheet."

A very well-known Good Friday service is the devotion of the Three Hours (*Tre Ore*). It was first performed in Lima, Peru, by Father Alphonso Messia, S.J. (1732), and quickly spread to all the Latin-speaking countries.[44] In Italy it was introduced with special enthusiasm, and from there came to England and this country, where in recent years it has grown in popularity also in many Protestant churches. It consists of sermons on the seven last words of Christ, alternating with hymns and prayers. It is usually held from noon until three o'clock on Good Friday. In France, Canada, and central Europe, the Three Hours' devotion is hardly known. Instead, oratorios on the seven words are often presented by church choirs in a musical service on Good Friday night. Such musical programs are also observed in many Protestant churches, both in Europe and America.

A famous feature of Good Friday is the popular procession in the Latin countries. In many regions, especially in Spain, the confraternities (*confradias*) of lay people, wearing hoods and carrying lighted candles, walk through the streets in religious parades. Images of the suffering Christ and the Blessed Virgin are conveyed in a pageant of magnificent splendor. The statues, borne on huge platforms, are beautifully decorated and surrounded by a multitude of burning tapers. In Malta the bearers wear oriental robes, and many go barefoot in observance of vows.

This Spanish custom of the *confradia* processions, especially the famous tradition of the city of Seville, has also found its way into the Spanish-speaking countries of the New World. Among the most impressive celebrations of this kind is the annual *Semana Santa* (Holy Week) observance in Mexico City. During the last three days before Easter, thousands throng the streets to watch the slow and solemn processions wind their way through the public thoroughfares. Life-size statues of Christ and Mary are borne on huge platforms surmounted by gorgeous canopies. Many dozens of electric candles are arranged on the platform, enveloping the images with a halo of soft light. The statues, robed in splendid gowns according to Spanish custom, are decorated with jewelry and with richly embroidered trains of silk or brocade.

Of the many men who carry the heavy platform, a good number walk barefoot in token of penance and reverence. In front and behind the statue march the members of the *confradia*, dressed in the gowns and colors of their pious association, their heads hooded, many of them carrying wooden crosses on their shoulders, others walking barefoot or in sandals. Some processions remain in deep silence, others recite the Rosary or march to the lugubrious strains of funeral music. To any stranger who has witnessed these *confradia* celebrations, the memory of them will remain an unforgettable experience of traditional Latin devotion.

In Mexico a funeral procession (*el santo entierro*) is held with a touching scene in which the mother of the Lord meets the lifeless body of her Son (*el pésame*). The Stations of the Cross are often dramatically represented in a passion play outside the church, followed by sermon and prayer. In parts of South America a procession, carrying the empty cross and many statues, moves slowly through the crowded church while the people pray and sing. In Caracas, Venezuela, this service is supposed to last four to five hours; and in order to fill the time, the procession not only moves very slowly but proceeds in a quaint manner, walking three steps forward and two steps backward. In India the native Christians accompany the "funeral" of Christ, which is met outside the church by a statue of the sorrowful Virgin. A sermon is preached, and both statues together are brought back into the church. There the people perform the *purana*, a service of wailing, at which they sing hymns to their ancient, plaintive tunes. The early missionaries to India were Portuguese, and naturally brought their native customs along with them.

Following the Reformation, the practice grew in Germany of presenting, on Good Friday afternoon, in place of the ancient liturgical service, musical settings of the parts of the Gospel narrating the Passion and death of Christ. One of the earliest works of this kind is the composition of Antonio Scandello (1580), choir director of the court chapel at Dresden. He wrote a *St. John's Passion* that follows the traditional recitative of the liturgical chant in the solo part (evangelist). He is the first composer to set the story of the Passion to music in oratorio form, and it became the model for most of his successors for hundreds of years.

Heinrich Schuetz (1672) set to dramatic music all four Gospel narrations of the Passion. They all close with a devotional chorus in motet style based on some familiar church hymn.

The best known and perhaps the greatest of all are the two immortal compositions of Johann Sebastian Bach, *Saint John Passion* and *Saint Matthew Passion*. The *Saint John Passion* was first performed on Good Friday, 1723, at Leipzig. Its first complete American performance was given by the Bach Choir of Bethlehem, Pennsylvania, in 1888. The *Saint Matthew Passion*, somewhat longer, was also produced for the first time in Leipzig, in 1729. During Passiontide throughout the world many performances of both these famous compositions are heard by thousands, especially since the advent of radio and television.

While Handel, at the age of nineteen, wrote a Passion (1704), far better known is his inspired *Messiah*. The latter half of this gigantic oratorio deals with the Crucifixion and Resurrection.

A composition of the *Seven Last Words* for solo, chorus, and orchestra was written by Franz Josef Haydn (1809) at the request of the Cathedral Chapter of Cadiz, Spain, to be performed at the Three Hours' devotion, and is being heard rather frequently in recent years.

The *Christus am Oelberg* (Christ on the Mount of Olives) by Beethoven, Charles Gounod's *Seven*

124

Last Words, César Franck's *Redemption* with a text by Eduard Blau are some of the many works of music for Passiontide. Gounod's *Seven Last Words* is often performed in both Catholic and Protestant churches on Good Friday.

A composition which in recent years has become a favorite with church choirs is the dramatic setting of the *Seven Last Words,* with a Latin text, by the French organist and composer Theodore Dubois (1924). It was first performed in Paris in 1869, and is now often given as a sacred concert on Palm Sunday evening or at some other time during Holy Week.

Some of the best-known works of English composers often heard in Protestant churches during Holy Week include: Maunder's *Olivet to Calvary,* Gaul's *Holy City,* and Stainer's *Crucifixion.*

Parsifal by Richard Wagner (1883), based on a folklore interpretation of the search for the Holy Grail, is an opera frequently heard in Holy Week, and the music for the "Good Friday Spell" from it is usually played by symphony orchestras here and in Europe during that period.

Following the spirit of the liturgy, the faithful everywhere keep Good Friday as a day of strictest fast, often far beyond the obligation of the law. Many

125

people take nothing but a little bread and water all day. In some counties of England plain rice cooked in milk is the traditional Good Friday meal. The Irish people hold a "black fast," which usually means that they take only water or tea on that day. In central Europe it is the custom to eat just vegetable soup and bread at noon, and some cheese with bread in the evening. Both meals are taken standing and in silence. No noisy tasks are performed, people refrain from joking and laughing, and children abstain from their usual games.

In many countries, pious legends have inspired popular practices that are widely observed, mostly in a spirit of true reverence, some of which, however, have given rise to superstitions. Among the farmers, Good Friday is considered a lucky day for sowing, since Christ blessed and sanctified the soil by His burial. On the other hand, craftsmen must be careful not to swing a hammer or drive a nail on the day on which Christ was nailed to the Cross; carpenters, plumbers, blacksmiths rest from their usual work. No washing is done by the women, since the Lord's blood stained the linen and clothes on Good Friday. A familiar superstition is that if a woman washes on Good Friday, she will find the laundry spotted with blood, and ill luck will befall her all through the year.

In Sussex, England, marbles was the popular game for both young boys and old men in many little country towns on Good Friday. No one would dream of neglecting to play marbles on this particular day. They would play beside the church gate in the street until it was time for the service to begin, and then continue with their game after the services were over. In fact, many who never played marbles at any other time during the year would try their hand at it on this day. One writer has suggested that originally it signified the throwing of dice at the foot of the Cross by the Roman soldiers for our Lord's robes and had perhaps been, before the Reformation, part of an early religious drama. Another odd custom in Brighton, England, used to be the sight of occupants of a whole fishing village skipping rope from dawn to dusk on Good Friday, which was called Hand Rope Day.

A deeply impressive practice among the Christian Syrians and Chaldeans is the fact that they do not use their customary greeting, *Shlama* ("Peace be with you") on Good Friday and Holy Saturday, because Judas Iscariot saluted Christ with these very words when he betrayed Him. Instead, they substitute on these two days, as mutual greeting, the

127

phrase, "The Light of God be with your departed ones."

It was a universal custom (and still is in Catholic countries) to mark a new loaf of bread with the sign of the cross before cutting it, in order to bless it and thank God for it. On special occasions the cross was imprinted on the loaf before baking, as on the Christmas loaves in southern France and in Greece, the *Kreuzstollen* (cross loaf) in Germany, the cross bread of Mid-Lent among the Slavs. On Good Friday, loaves bearing an imprinted cross are eaten in Austria (*Karfreitaglaib*). In England, from the end of the fourteenth century, buns were baked with a cross marked on them. They are said to have originated at Saint Alban's Abbey in 1361, where the monks distributed them to the poor. Whatever their origin, these "hot cross buns" became a famous Good Friday feature in England and Ireland, and later in this country. They were made of spiced dough, round in shape, with a cross made of icing on the top. Two "royal bun houses" in the Chelsea district of London turned them out by the thousands on Good Friday morning. There was a flat-roofed wooden piazza running along the whole front of these famous bun houses beneath which the hundreds of customers were protected "from summer's heat and winter's cold," as they shoved and pushed their way to the trays containing "royal hot Chelsea buns" offered for sale. Those who really knew their buns gave preference to the "old original royal bun house" at which "the king himself once stopped." In recent times, however, just as Christmas has begun to be celebrated practically the day after Thanksgiving in this country, so the note of commercialism has crept into bun eating, and they are now purchasable not just significantly on Good Friday but throughout Lent. Long ago they were also sold by street vendors singing rhymes, such as this:

Hot cross buns, hot cross buns,
One a penny, two a penny,
Hot cross buns.
   If your daughters won't eat them,
   Give them to your sons;
   But if you have none of those little elves,
   Then you must eat them all yourselves.

Poor Robin's Almanack, 1733, gives this version:

Good Friday comes this month, the old woman runs
With one or two a penny hot cross-buns,
Whose virtue is, if you believe what's said,
They'll not grow mouldy like the common bread.

In ancient times the hot cross buns were considered blessed and powerful against all kinds of sick-

129

ness and dangers. Eating them on Good Friday was said to protect your home from fire. People would keep them through the year, eating them as medicine or wearing them as charms against disease, lightning, and shipwreck.

In many parts of Europe people who die on Good Friday are considered highly fortunate, since they are believed to share in the privilege of the Good Thief, and to be given the grace of salvation and a speedy entry into Heaven.

Among the numerous popular legends connected with our Lord's death, the most notable one is that of the Holy Grail. Joseph of Arimathea, so the story goes, acquired the chalice that Christ had used at the Last Supper. In this cup he gathered the blood which dripped from the holy wounds when the sacred body was taken down from the Cross. After the Resurrection, the Holy Grail was brought by angels to Europe where it is kept in the church of a secret castle that stands majestically on the peak of a high and hidden mountain. There it is venerated and guarded by angels, priests, and knights. Medieval literature abounds with legendary epics and stories of the Grail and of knights who went in quest of it.[45]

CHAPTER 11

Holy Saturday

The English title for the day before Easter, Holy Saturday, is a translation of its official name in the Western Church—*Sabbatum Sanctum*. In the Oriental Church they call it the "Sacred and Great Saturday." Most European nations use the term "holy," except in parts of eastern Europe, where the term "the Great Saturday" is in vogue. The German people say "Saturday of mourning" (*Karsamstag*). On the Island of Malta, where Arabic is spoken, Holy Saturday bears the name *Sibt il Glorja* (Saturday of Glory). The Christians in Iraq and Iran employ the popular term *Sabt al-Noor* (Saturday of Light).

The original observance of Holy Saturday commemorated Christ's rest in the tomb. In the early Church there was no service at all during the daylight hours, since the body of the Lord enclosed in the Sepulcher shared the fate and humiliation of human burial. Just as Christ rested in the grave the whole Sabbath day, so the faithful waited in prayer until the evening star announced the beginning of the Easter vigil.

In ancient days a strict fast called the "Passion fast" was kept until the morning of Easter Sunday; not even children were dispensed from observing it. Both the Eastern and Western Churches called Holy Saturday the "Day of Rest of the Lord's Body in the Tomb." In the fourteenth century the original night service of the Easter vigil was transferred to the morning of Holy Saturday, but in 1951 Pope Pius XII tentatively restored the ancient custom, and it is once more held as a Holy Saturday night service, leading directly into Easter Sunday.

In the early centuries the catechumens would assemble in the church during the afternoon, the men on one side, the women on the other. After an instruction by the bishop, the priests performed on them those rites which are still practiced in the baptism of infants and adults: the exorcism of the powers of evil, the touching of ears and nostrils as a symbol

132

of opening their minds to the word and grace of God, and the solemn pledge of conversion. This pledge was accompanied by a dramatic gesture—turning toward the west and pointing with the forefinger in the direction of sunset, each catechumen uttered these words, "I renounce thee, Satan, with all thy pomps and all thy works," then turning to the east and pointing likewise, they would say, "To Thee I dedicate myself, Jesus Christ, eternal and uncreated Light." After this each one recited the Creed publicly before the whole congregation; then they were dismissed to spend the last few hours before their baptism in quiet recollection and prayer.

On Holy Saturday in all cities and towns the mood of quiet, somber expectancy suddenly turned into radiant exultation and joy at the sight of the first evening stars. Thousands of lights began to illuminate the growing darkness. The churches seemed to burst with the blaze of lamps and candles, the homes of the people shone with light, and even the streets were bright with the glow of a thousand tapers. At a time when electric lights were unknown, this tremendous annual illumination was overwhelming. The deep impressions it created are still reflected in the writings of the Fathers and in the text of our liturgical service. The night was called the "mother of all holy vigils," [46] the "great service of light" (*sacrum lucernarium*), the "night of radiant splendor" (*irradiata fulgoribus*), the "night of illumination" (*luminosa haec nox*). We are told that Emperor Constantine (331) "transformed the night of the sacred vigil into the brilliance of day, by lighting throughout the whole city [of Milan] pillars of wax, while burning lamps illuminated every house, so that this nocturnal celebration was rendered brighter than the brightest day." [47] Saint Gregory of Nyssa (394), in one of his Easter sermons, mentions "this glowing night which links the splendor of burning lamps to the morning rays of the sun, thus producing continuous daylight without any darkness." [48]

Many hymns have been written in praise of this illumination on the vigil of Easter, the best known being the poem *Inventor rutilis* written by Prudentius (405), a layman and government official of the Roman Empire, and a great Christian poet:

> Eternal God, O Lord of Light,
> Who hast created day and night:
> The sun has set, and shadows deep
> Now over land and waters creep;
> But darkness must not reign today:
> Grant us the light of Christ, we pray.

It is difficult to picture today the solemn joy and excitement that filled the hearts of Christians in the early centuries on that night. For them the Easter vigil was the glorious annual triumph which they celebrated together with Christ over sin, death, and the powers of evil. Their excitement was increased beyond modern comprehension by the universal belief in those days that Christ would return for the Last Judgment during one of these Easter vigils. Nobody stayed at home, not even the little children. The multitudes crowded into the churches; and thousands thronged around the house of God, joining in prayer with those who had been fortunate enough to find places inside. Gold and silver candelabra shed their cheerful light through the open doors and windows, hundreds of lamps suspended from the ceiling illumined the church with a new splendor.

The custom of spending the Easter vigil in prayer seems to date from the very time of the apostles. Tertullian called it an "ancient ordination," and remarked that nobody could be exempted from it. Its origin, he said, was so old that its beginnings were unknown even in his time (third century). The vigil service began with the blessing and lighting of the paschal candle, which from the earliest period was considered a sacred symbol of Christ's person. The *praeconia paschalia* (jubilant Easter songs) which accompanied the lighting of the candle were already performed in the Roman Empire at the end of the

135

fourth century. The earliest manuscript containing the present text of the song (*Exultet*) dates from the seventh or eighth century. After the blessing of the candle, a prayer service was held; passages of the Bible were read (the "prophecies"), then the priests and people recited psalms, antiphons, and orations. This service lasted much longer than today, but the faithful did not mind, since they spent the whole night in church anyway.

Toward midnight the bishop and clergy went in procession to the baptismal font, a large basin built in a structure outside the church. There the baptismal water was consecrated with the prayers and ceremonies still in use today. Once more the catechumens were addressed by their spiritual shepherd. Then, divested of any ornaments or jewelry, they stepped into the "life-giving waters." The bishop, also standing in the water, baptized them one by one, first the men, then the women and children. After baptism they were anointed. Finally they put on sandals and flowing white garments of pure linen. In this attire they appeared at all services until the end of Easter Week.

Long after midnight, probably at the first dawn of Easter Sunday, the vigil was concluded with the customary prayers of the litanies and celebration of the vigil Mass, at which the newly baptized Christians received their first Communion.

This basic structure of the ancient Easter vigil is still preserved in the ceremonies of Holy Saturday, though some rites have been added in the course of centuries. Earlier, only tapers and lamps were used as symbols of the light and life of our Lord's Resurrection, but a notable new rite is the blessing of the Easter fire.

The Germanic nations had a popular tradition of setting big bonfires at the beginning of spring. This custom was frowned upon by the Church because it served a pagan symbolism, and consequently was suppressed when those nations became Christian. As late as 742, at the Synod of Mainz, the prohibition of such fires was firmly upheld. A probable explanation of how these fires were finally admitted and acknowledged by the Church is the fact that the Irish bishops and monks who came to the European continent in the sixth and seventh centuries had brought with them an ancient rite of their own: the setting and blessing of big bonfires outside the church on Holy Saturday night. Saint Patrick himself, the Father and Founder of the Church in Ireland, had started this tradition, to supplant the Druidic pagan spring fires with a Christian and religious fire symbol of Christ, the light of the world.[49]

This Christian usage of an Easter bonfire naturally appealed to the population of the West-Frankish Kingdom (France), where the Irish monks established flourishing monasteries. In the East-Frankish Kingdom (Germany) the Easter fires remained suppressed for a long time, mostly because the missionaries of those regions had not come from Ireland but from England, and thus did not know the custom of a Christian Easter fire. Finally Pope Zachary (752) gave his approval for the "toleration" of the practice. This tolerated custom became so popular eventually that the popes incorporated it into the liturgy of the Western Church in the latter part of the ninth century. Thus it seems that the blessing of the Easter fire, originated by Saint Patrick, has now become the opening rite of the liturgical ceremonies on Holy Saturday.

A similar rite, which has no historical connection with the blessing of the Easter fire, is the famous "Holy fire" that is produced every year on Holy Saturday morning in the shrine of the Sepulcher at Jerusalem. The Greek (Orthodox) Patriarch of the Holy City enters the Lord's tomb, and after a short while hands a burning taper out of the enclosure. A shouting, jubilant multitude receives this light, which is shared among the crowd from candle to candle. Flames of the Holy fire are carried by young men to

138

the churches of Bethlehem and Nazareth. Up to World War I the fire also was brought by boat to Odessa and from there distributed throughout Russia. An ancient popular legend asserts that this fire comes down from Heaven every year and miraculously kindles the brand in the tomb of the Savior. The first description of the ceremony of the Holy fire dates from the beginning of the twelfth century; since then it has not changed in any major detail, except that it is now held under the auspices of the Greek Orthodox Church, while in past centuries the Catholic Patriarch used to perform it.

The Apostolic Creed contains the phrase, "He descended into Hell" (*descendit ad inferos*). This means that the Soul of Christ, after His death, announced to the souls of the just the accomplished redemption which opened for them the gates of eternal bliss. Christian piety has adorned this historical fact with dramatic descriptions of the Lord's victory over Satan: He appears in the glory of His divine majesty, illuminating the kingdom of darkness and breaking down the gates of Hell. He binds Satan and releases the souls of the patriarchs from their long imprisonment. A multitude of pictures, hymns, sermons, and dramatic representations in medieval times had this "Harrowing of Hell" as their subject. The familiar pictures of the Risen Christ, holding aloft the banner

139

of victory over death and devil, also were inspired by this article of faith.

A former rite performed in Rome on the morning of Holy Saturday since the fifth century was the making and blessing of the Agnus Dei (Lamb of God) at the Lateran Church. The archdeacon, melting wax, mixed it with chrism (consecrated oil), blessed it, and poured the mixture into small oval molds which bore the imprint of the liturgical symbol of the Lamb (representing Christ, the Lamb of God). These Agnus Dei were later distributed to the faithful as souvenirs of the feast and as sacramentals, through the devout use of which the protection and blessing of God in various needs of body and soul would be obtained. In recent centuries this rite is performed every five years by the Pope himself. He then distributes the Agnus Dei on Saturday of Easter Week in the Sistine Chapel.

In medieval times it was a general custom to celebrate the *Elevatio* (Raising) of the sacred Host or the cross from the shrine of the Sepulcher during the night of Holy Saturday or in the early morning of Easter Sunday. In many places this was done by the clergy alone. A procession would bear the Blessed Sacrament or the cross from the shrine to the main altar. A more solemn variety of this custom is the Resurrection service, still widely practiced in central

Europe. On the evening of Holy Saturday, with the church already decorated for Easter, the priest takes the Blessed Sacrament from the shrine, removes the white veil, and holding the monstrance aloft intones the ancient antiphon, "The Lord is risen, alleluia." While the faithful sing their traditional Easter songs and all the church bells ring, the procession moves from the shrine to the main altar. There the *Te Deum* is intoned, and a solemn benediction concludes the inspiring service.

Christian folklore has adorned Holy Saturday with a wealth of interesting customs, most of them based on the joyful liturgy of the anticipated Easter vigil. In many sections of Europe the vigil lights at the domestic shrines are extinguished early in the morning. No fire or light is allowed anywhere in the house. The stoves, lamps, and candlesticks have been cleaned and prepared on the preceding days; now they stand ready to receive the blessed fire. Meanwhile the boys build a pile of wooden logs in front of the church, each contributing a piece to which a strand of wire is fastened. At this pile the priest strikes the Easter fire and blesses it. As log after log begins to burn, the youngsters draw them out and rush home swinging the glowing pieces. From them the lamps and the stove are lit. Then the faggots are extinguished and put aside; pieces will be placed

141

in the kitchen stove when storms and lightning threaten throughout the year.

In other places people carry the flames of the blessed fire in lanterns back to their homes. A vigil light before the crucifix is lit, and zealously guarded all through the year.

At the moment of the Gloria in the Mass, when suddenly all the bells start ringing again, the people who have to stay at home embrace and wish each other a blessed Easter. From this moment, too, musical instruments may again be played, and the children are allowed to resume their noisy games and to eat candy and sweets which they have "given up" during the past three days.

On Holy Saturday there is great activity around the house in central Europe. Easter ham and other foods for the feast are cooked in the kitchen, Easter bread and pastry are baked. Many eggs are boiled and painted. The whole house is decked with flowers and finery. A festive mood prevails. In the Slavic countries, baskets of food, especially eggs, are brought to the church to be blessed by the priest on Holy Saturday afternoon. They are then taken home and eaten for breakfast on Easter Sunday, Monday, and Tuesday. In many regions the priests go from house to house on Holy Saturday to bless the Easter fare which is neatly arranged on large tables and decorated with flowers. All those who come to visit are offered an Easter egg.

The Roman ritual provides a special blessing of food at Easter. The Poles, however, have their own traditional formulas of blessing, authorized by the Synod of Piotrkow (fifteenth century) and approved by Rome. Here is an ancient Polish Easter blessing:

O Lord, who hast blessed five loaves in the desert, graciously give us bread for life's needs.

Almighty God, let not your gifts lead us to sin. Let not the goblet of sparkling wine induce us to misdeeds.

While we enjoy our feast, let us also in charity remember all those who suffer want and hunger.

May not the pleasure of the body stifle the inspirations of thy Holy Spirit, o Lord.

Before the present regime in Russia it was the custom after midnight benediction on Holy Saturday night to bless the *paska* (the Easter bread), which is really a small saffron cake, a miniature pyramid consisting of stiff curds and egg products. The *paska* having been carried to the priest to be blessed was then brought back to the home and given a place of honor on the Easter breakfast table. Easter was always the great day in Russia for exchanging gifts. It was made the same sort of festivity as ours with Christmas presents. In addition to their joy over the

143

Resurrection of our Lord and their own spiritual awakening, the Russian people at this season of the year used to thank God for the beginning of the disappearance of the snow and ice of their long bitter winters.

An amusing custom is practiced in Poland on Holy Saturday morning. The boys of the villages "bury" the Lenten fare, herring and *zur,* in a mock funeral. The herring (a real one or a wooden image) is first executed by hanging, then a pot of *zur* is shattered against a rock or tree; finally the fish and the pieces of the pot are interred with glee. No longer will these tiresome dishes be eaten, at least not until next Lent.

In the Alpine provinces of Austria, Easter fires burn on mountain peaks after sunset on Holy Saturday. Many bands of musicians go through the valleys playing ancient hymns and singing Easter carols to the sound of guitars. Children accompany them carrying lighted torches, and join in the singing.

CHAPTER 12

The Feast of Feasts

"This is the day which the Lord has made, the Feast of Feasts, and our Pasch: the Resurrection of our Savior Jesus Christ according to the flesh." With these solemn words the official calendar of the Western Church announces the celebration of Easter. Equally solemn are the words of the calendar (*Pentecostarion*) of the Eastern Church: "The sacred and great Sunday of the Pasch, on which we celebrate the lifegiving Resurrection of our Lord and God, the Savior Jesus Christ."

The joy and exultation over this greatest of all Christian feasts is evident in the writings of the

145

Saints and Fathers from earliest times. Easter is referred to as the "peak (*akropolis*) of all Feasts" and
the "Queen of all solemnities." Saint Gregory of
Nazianz (390) writes, "This highest Feast and greatest celebration so much surpasses not only civic holidays but also the other feast days of the Lord, that
it is like the sun among stars." [50]

This feast is called Pasch by most nations: Greeks
and Rumanians (*Pascha*), Italians (*Pasqua*), Span-
iards and Portuguese (*Pascua*), French (*Pâque*),
Norwegians (*Paskir*), Danes (*Paaske*), Gaels (*casc*).
As stated before, this word is taken from the Greek
(and Latin) "pascha" which comes from the Hebrew
word *pesach* (passover). The Passover was celebrated by the Jews on the fourteenth day of the
month *Nisan,* which began about a week before the
full moon of spring. It was instituted to commemorate the deliverance of the people of Israel the night
before their departure from Egypt. The angel of God
destroyed the firstborn of Egypt but passed over
the houses of the Israelites. It was the command of
God, announced by Moses, that each Hebrew family should slay a young lamb without blemish, and
sprinkle its blood on the frame of the door. In the
evening the lamb was to be roasted, no bones were
to be broken, and it was to be eaten with unleavened
bread and bitter herbs by all members of the family.

146

According to Divine ordination, this rite was to be repeated every year in a solemn ceremony on the eve of the feast, and is still celebrated by Jewish people everywhere today. Jesus observed it for the last time on the night before He died.

There is a significant link between the Jewish Passover and the Christian Easter, because Christ died on Passover Day. It is also symbolic, because the lamb that had to be sacrificed for the deliverance of Israel is considered by the Church as prophetic of Him who is the "Lamb of God, who takes away the sins of the world" (John 1, 29). Thus the name and meaning of the Hebrew Pasch was devoutly accepted into the Christian liturgy. Although the death and Resurrection of the Redeemer would have been commemorated by Christians at whatever time they might have occurred, it is of special significance that the Lord actually did die and rise during the days of the Passover celebration.

From the very first, the Resurrection of Christ was celebrated as the greatest and most important festive day of the whole year. In fact, every Sunday is a "little Easter" consecrated to the memory of the Risen Christ. In the Eastern Churches, Sunday bears the name "Resurrection" even today. The Council of Nicaea (325) prescribed that on Sundays and during Easter time all Christians should pray standing, never to bend their knees, to indicate "that we are risen with Christ." A relic of this custom is the practice of saying the *Angelus* (daily prayer commemorating the incarnation) standing, instead of kneeling, on Sundays and at Easter time. Most people are familiar with Millet's famous painting "The Angelus," depicting the peasant farmer and wife standing in their field at prayer.

In addition to this weekly celebration of Christ's Resurrection, the Church has observed each year from the earliest centuries a special feast at the time of the Jewish Pasch, to commemorate the anniversary of the greatest events in the Christian world. Since there is an intimate bond between the Resurrection of Christ and the sacrament of baptism, the Church united these two "resurrections" in a common ritual. She celebrates the "new life" not only of Christ as the Head, but also of his mystical body, his faithful followers. This is why the prayers of the liturgy in paschal week constantly reflect those two thoughts: the Resurrection of our Lord and the baptism of the faithful.

The English word "Easter" and the German *Ostern* come from a common origin (*Eostur, Eastur, Ostara, Ostar*), which to the Norsemen meant the season of the rising (growing) sun, the season of new birth.

148

The word was used by our ancestors to designate the "Feast of New Life" in the spring. The same root is found in the name for the place where the sun rises (East, *Ost*). The word Easter, then, originally meant the celebration of the spring sun which had its birth in the East and brought new life upon earth. This symbolism was transferred to the supernatural meaning of our Easter, to the new life of the Risen Christ, the eternal and uncreated Light.

Based on a passage in the writings of Saint Bede the Venerable (735), the term "Easter" has often been explained as the name of an Anglo-Saxon goddess (*Eostre*),[51] though no such goddess is known in the mythologies of any Germanic tribe. Modern research has made it quite clear that Saint Bede erroneously interpreted the name of the season as that of a goddess.

Some Slavic nations like the Poles call Easter the "Great Night," (*Wielkanoc*); the Ukrainians, Russians, Serbs, say the "Great Day" (*Velik Den*). In Hungary it is referred to as "Feast of Meat" (*Husvet*), because the eating of meat is resumed again after the long fast.

In medieval documents Easter is often recorded as the beginning of a new year, especially in France where this custom prevailed until 1563. At Easter time the Roman Emperors, starting with Valentinian

149

in 367, released from prison persons who were not dangerous criminals; this practice was followed by emperors, kings, and popes all through medieval times and up to the present century.

An interesting example is recorded in the diary of an English traveler of the seventeenth century. He reported that during a service at Easter time in one of the Roman churches he saw a boy seated on a chair next to the altar; the youngster was dressed in a blue robe, wore a wreath of olive twigs on his head, and held a burning candle in his hand. He was a lad of about fifteen who had been committed to prison for killing another boy, and by the Pope's order been freed in honor of Easter.[52]

Leading citizens in the Roman Empire imitated the clemency of the emperors at Easter time, granting freedom to slaves, forgiving enemies by ending feuds and quarrels, and discontinuing prosecutions in the courts as well. These customs, too, prevailed all through medieval times in the Christian countries of Europe.

A reverent and endearing practice is the combined Easter greeting and Easter kiss. In the early centuries, the faithful embraced each other with the words, *"Surrexit Dominus vere"* (Christ is truly risen), to which the answer was, *"Deo gratias"* (Thanks be to God). In the Greek Church the greeting is, *"Christos aneste"* (Christ is risen), the answer, *"Alethos aneste"* (He is truly risen). This greeting is still generally used by the Russians and Ukrainians (*Christos voskres—vo istinu voskres*).

In Russia the Easter kiss was bestowed during Matins before the night Mass; the people would embrace each other in the church. All through Easter Week the mutual kiss and embrace were repeated, not only in the homes, but also on the streets, even to strangers. The Poles and Western Slavs greet each other with the wish, "A joyful alleluia to you!" (*Wesolego Alleluja*).

In medieval times, when the bishop celebrated Easter Mass in his cathedral and the clergy received Communion from his hand, the priests and ministers would kiss him on the cheek after Communion, according to the regulations. At Saint Peter's in Rome, on Easter Sunday before High Mass, the Pope embraces the three youngest Cardinals who meet him as he approaches the altar.

Another ancient rite of Easter is the solemn Easter Communion. Church law requires the reception of the Holy Eucharist at least once a year, during Easter time. This edict dates from the fourth Council of the Lateran (1215). The law was not made to inaugurate a new practice but to safeguard the minimum demands of an old tradition. In the early centuries a

151

great deal more was expected from the faithful than Communion only once a year. The Council of Agde (506), for instance, had urged all Christians to receive at least three times a year.

In the beginning, the obligation of Easter Communion had to be fulfilled on the feast day itself. However, the Church gradually extended the time of this obligation, which now begins on Ash Wednesday and closes on Sunday after Pentecost (Trinity Sunday).

CHAPTER 13

Easter Sunday

The solemn services in honor of Christ's Resurrection
begin at midnight in the Greek Church. The priest
and all the congregation, lighted candles in hand,
leave the church by a side door after the vigil of
Easter. The procession walks around to the main
door, which has been closed (representing the sealed
tomb of Christ). The priest slowly makes the sign
of the cross with the crucifix he holds in his right
hand. At this moment the doors swing open, the
people intone the hymn, "Christ Is Risen," all the
church bells start pealing, and the jubilant procession
moves into the brightly illuminated church. The

candles in the hands of the worshipers fill the building with a sea of sparkling lights. The Matins of Easter are then sung, and the Holy Sacrifice of the Mass, at which all present receive Communion, is celebrated.

After Mass the solemn Easter blessing is bestowed upon the food brought by each family. Nobody would think of eating unblessed food at Easter. In the cities of Russia this blessing used to be held outside the church. People would pile the food on tables, around their Easter cakes; each cake bore a lighted taper. The priests in their resplendent robes, accompanied by assistants, passed in procession beside the waiting multitude, blessing the food and the people as bells rang and the church choir intoned joyous Easter hymns.

In the Latin Church there are no special ceremonies other than the Mass itself, which is celebrated in all churches with festive splendor and great solemnity.

Of particular historical interest is the liturgical sequence (hymn after the Gradual of the Mass). The sequences originated in the tenth century as Latin texts to be substituted for the long-drawn final "a" of the alleluia which is sung at the end of the Gradual.

The sequence of Easter Sunday, *Victimae Paschali*

Laudes (Praise to the Paschal Victim) was written
by the priest Wipo (about 1030), court chaplain of
Emperor Conrad. It soon became part of the official
text of the Easter Mass and is sung or recited in all
Catholic churches every day during Easter Week.

The significant fact is that the *Victimae Paschali*
was the first inspiration for the famous miracle plays
that developed into a wealth of religious drama from
the tenth century on. All dramatic performances of
sacred subjects, both within and without the
churches, are traced back to this Easter sequence.
The dramatic question and answer structure of
Wipo's poem lent itself naturally to this lovely scene:

Tell us, Maria, what didst thou see on thy way?
  I saw the tomb of the living Christ
  And the glory of the Risen Lord,
  The angels who gave witness,
  The winding-sheet and the linen cloths.
  Christ, my Hope, is risen!
  He precedes you into Galilee.
Now we truly know that Christ is risen from the dead.
Thou, Victor, Savior-King, have mercy on us.
                              Amen. Alleluia.

The words of Wipo's text were soon amplified by
other phrases from the Bible; and the appealing play
was eventually presented with appropriate devotion
before the shrine of the Sepulcher on Easter Sunday

morning. It was called "The Visit to the Tomb" (*Visitatio sepulcri*). In front of the shrine, now empty (the cross or Blessed Sacrament having been removed), the clergy played the scene of the Gospel that tells of the visit of the holy women to the tomb on Sunday morning. Two young clerics in white gowns, who sat or stood at the shrine, represented the angels and pronounced the Easter message at the end of the play: "He is not here, He is risen as He foretold. Go, tell His disciples that He is risen. Alleluia."

These liturgical Easter plays strongly appealed to the devout in medieval centuries. As time went on, various plays were written for Christmas, Epiphany, and other feast days. They all followed the structure of the Easter play inspired by the *Victimae Paschali*. A large number of these Easter plays, and later similar Christmas and Epiphany plays, are preserved in manuscripts and early prints all over Europe as well as in some of the museums and private collections in this country.

Special celebrations were held in most countries of Europe during the early morning hours of Easter Sunday. According to legend all running water was blessed with great powers to protect and heal. In rural sections the inhabitants still perform various water rites at the dawn of the feast. In Austria,

156

groups of young people gather long before sunrise
in meadows or on hilltops to dance traditional Easter
dances and sing their ancient carols. Here is the text
and music of one such old song:

This is now indeed a most heavenly night,
The Savior is risen in glory and light;
He rose when dawn was approaching soon.

All things do rejoice on this morning so fair;
The fire, the water, the soil and the air,
The stars above, and the paling moon.

So stand we and sing in the dawn's early glow,
Till Easter day brightens the valley below:
Hail, Christ, thou Light of eternal noon! [53]

A universal celebration was held in the Middle
Ages at the hour of sunrise. According to an old

157

legend, the sun dances on Easter morning or makes three cheerful jumps at the moment of rising, in honor of Christ's Resurrection. The rays of light penetrating the clouds were said to be angels dancing for joy. In Ireland and England people would put a pan of water in the east window and watch the dancing sun mirrored in it. The English poet Sir John Suckling (1641) refers to this custom in his *Ballad upon a Wedding:*

> Her feet beneath her petticoat
> Like little mice stole in and out,
>   As if they feared the light;
> But, oh, she dances such a way,
> No sun upon an Easter-day
>   Is half so fine a sight.

All over Europe people would gather in open plains or on the crests of hills to watch the spectacle of sunrise on Easter Day. The moment of daybreak was marked by the shooting of cannon and the ringing of bells. Bands and choirs used to greet the rising sun as a symbol of the Risen Christ with Easter hymns and alleluia songs. This morning salute is still performed in the Alpine regions of Austria.

On the island of Malta, a quaint custom is practiced at sunrise on Easter Day. A group of men carries a statue of the Savior from their church to a hilltop of the neighborhood, not in slow and solemn procession but *running* uphill as fast as they can, to indicate the motion of rising.

In most places the crowds would pray as the sun appeared; often this prayer service was led by the priest, and the whole group would afterward go in procession to the parish church for Easter Mass. From this medieval custom dates our modern sunrise service held by many congregations in this country on Easter Sunday. One of the oldest of these services, which has preserved the character of medieval tradition, is held annually at Bethlehem, Pennsylvania, among the Moravians. At three o'clock in the morning a band, playing Easter hymns, awakens the sleepers. An hour later they gather in large numbers at the church yard to celebrate the Resurrection with prayer and singing until the sun rises and a church service ends the impressive solemnity.

As the newly baptized Christians in the early centuries wore white garments of new linen, so it became a tradition among all the faithful to appear in new clothes on Easter Sunday, symbolizing the "new life" that the Lord, through His Resurrection, bestowed upon all believers. This custom was widespread during medieval times; in many places a popular superstition threatened with ill luck all those who could afford to buy new clothes for Easter Sun-

159

day but refused to do so. It is an ancient saying in Connemara, Ireland: "For Christmas, food and drink; for Easter, new clothes." On Easter many children in Ireland dress in green, white, and yellow: green hair ribbons, yellow dress, and white shoes. It is also an old tradition for some children there to wear little crosses made of multicolored ribbons on the right arm on Easter Sunday (perhaps a substitute for those who cannot afford new clothes). This ancient tradition of new clothes is still adhered to, although its meaning and background have long since been forgotten by many. Actually, in many a modern family this is, perhaps, the one and only Easter custom that is still faithfully practiced.

Another picturesque old Easter Sunday custom is the "Easter walk" through fields and open spaces after Mass. This is still held in many parts of Europe. Dressed in their finery, the men and women, especially the younger ones, march in a well-ordered parade through the town and into the open country. A decorated crucifix or, in some places, the Easter candle is borne at the head of the procession. At certain points on the route they recite prayers and sing Easter hymns, interspersed with gay chatting along the way. In some parts of Germany and Austria, groups of young farmers ride on richly decorated horses (*Osterritt*). After the Reformation this medi-

160

eval Easter walk lost its original religious character and gradually developed into our present-day Easter parade.

One of the highlights of Easter in this country is, of course, New York's famous Fifth Avenue fashion parade, where for many years people from all walks of life have paraded their Easter finery after the Sunday morning church services. In late years many abuses have occurred, when press agents and publicity-seeking celebrities put on unbecoming stunts to attract the attention of the crowds. Things got so out of hand that now strict enforcement of proper behavior is in order, and no longer can sensation seekers make a field day out of this custom.

On Easter Sunday open house is held in most Christian nations. Relatives, neighbors, and friends exchange visits. Easter eggs and bunnies are the order of the day, and special Easter hams are the principal dish at dinner. In the rural parts of Austria, any stranger may freely enter any house on Easter Sunday; he will be welcomed by the host and may eat whatever Easter food he wishes. Among the Christians in the Near East the whole Sunday (after Mass and breakfast) is spent in visiting friends and neighbors; wine, pastry, and coffee are served, and children receive presents of eggs and sweets.

On Easter Sunday afternoon most people in the

161

villages and towns of central Europe come back to church for the solemn services of Vespers and Bene-diction. At the sermon that preceded this afternoon service, a quaint custom was practiced in those re-gions during medieval times. The priests would regale their congregations with funny stories and poems, drawing moral conclusions from these jolly tales (*Ostermärlein:* Easter fables). The purpose of this unusual practice was to reward the faithful with something gay after the many sad and serious Lenten preachings, a purpose easily achieved as the churches rang with the loud and happy laughter of the audi-ence (*risus paschalis:* Easter laughter). This tradi-tion is found as early as the thirteenth century. From the fourteenth to the eighteenth centuries the cus-tom was widespread, and a number of collections of Easter fables appeared in print.[54] The reformers violently attacked the practice as an abuse, however, and it was gradually suppressed by the Church dur-ing the seventeenth and eighteenth centuries.

It is an ancient custom in Slavic countries (Russia, Ukraine, Poland, etc.) to ring the church bells with short intervals all day from morning to night on Easter Sunday, reminding the faithful that it is the greatest feast of the year.

One of the most impressive Easter sights in the world, admired by people of all faiths, is the annual illumination of St. Peter's Church in Rome on the evening of the feast day. The whole majestic cathedral becomes a mass of flickering lights against the dark sky, every detail of its architectural structure outlined. From all parts of the city, but especially from the Pincio, tens of thousands watch this breathtaking, unforgettable sight in silence. After an hour or two, the lights slowly change to a reddish hue, and gradually fade away.

CHAPTER 14

Easter Hymns and Music

Ancient Easter songs, radiant in their simplicity, were the main source of inspiration for popular hymns of later times.

As early as the second century, the priest Melito of Sardes (Asia Minor) praised the Resurrection:

> Trembling for joy cries all creation;
> What is this mystery, so great and new?
> The Lord has risen from among the dead,
> And Death itself He crushed with valiant foot.
> Behold the cruel tyrant bound and chained,
> And man made free by Him who rose!

164

From the fourth century date the magnificent Latin hymns of Easter praise (*praeconium paschale*) which used to be sung at the lighting of the Easter candle. The *Exultet*, still sung in all Catholic churches during the liturgy of the Easter vigil, is a later formulation of such an ancient hymn. Its origin is unknown, although it has often been ascribed to Saint Jerome or to Saint Augustine. Here are a few lines:

This is the Night,
Which throughout the world
Frees all who believe in Christ
From the vices of their time-shackled existence,
From the lightless dungeon of sin,
And restores them to grace: unites them to holiness.

This is the Night
In which Christ broke the chains of death
And rose in radiant victory
From the pit of Hades.

Another fourth-century poem is the Latin hymn of Saint Ambrose, expressing the "paradox of faith" as seen in the death and Resurrection of Christ:

O mystery great and glorious,
That mortal flesh should conquer death,

165

And all our human pains and wounds
The Lord should heal by bearing them.

Behold how man, though crushed by death,
Now does arise and live with Christ,
While death, repelled and robbed of might,
Dies from its own malignant sting.

Early Christian hymns with similar thoughts were written by Saint Gregory of Nazianz and Bishop Synesios of Cyrene (about 414). Another hymn ascribed to Saint Ambrose is now used in the Lauds of Low Sunday: *Claro paschali gaudio.* An English translation may be found in the Protestant Episcopal hymnal of the United States ("That Easter Day with Joy Was Bright").

Venantius Fortunatus wrote (about 580) a Latin hymn, *Salve festa dies* (Hail, Festive Day!) which was later translated into various languages and became a popular Easter song. The first English translation is mentioned in a letter of Archbishop Cranmer to King Henry VIII, in 1544.

An ancient hymn now recited at Vespers during Easter time is the poem *Ad regias Agni dapes* (The Royal Banquet of the Lamb). The present version, based on the text of a sixth- or seventh-century unknown author, was rearranged for the breviary under Pope Urban VIII (1644).

Saint John Damascene (eighth century) wrote a number of beautiful Greek poems in honor of the Resurrection, some of which are now used in the liturgical services of the Greek Church, and have been translated into English and become popular Easter hymns:

"Thou Hallowed Chosen Morn of Praise" (*Aute he klete kai hagia hemera*). It is sung in the Greek liturgy during Easter night. A free English translation was published by John M. Neale in 1862; the tune for the English text is taken from a German melody composed by Johann H. Schein in 1628.

"Sing All Nations" (*Aidomen pantes laoi*). An English adaptation ("Come Ye Faithful, Raise the Strain of Triumphant Gladness") was published by Neale in 1859. The tune was adopted from a German song by Johann Horn, printed in Nürnberg in 1544.

"The Day of Resurrection" (*Anastaseos Hemera*) is sung in its original Greek text at the midnight service of the Greek Church, when the faithful light their candles before going to Communion. A free translation into English was written by Neale. It is sung to the tune of an old German Madonna hymn (*Ave Maria, klarer und lichter Morgenstern*) which appeared in 1784.[55]

From a German interpolation between the lines of the Easter sequence (*Victimae Paschali*) originated the famous hymn *"Christus ist erstanden"* (Christ Is

167

Risen) which is sung to a tune dating from the year 1531. This ancient song is still the most popular Easter hymn in both Catholic and Protestant churches in Germany. It is intoned by the priest and sung by the people at the solemn service of Resurrection (*Auferstehungsfeier*) on Holy Saturday night. An English text was written by Isaac Watts (1748).

Many beautiful Easter songs date from the later Middle Ages. A true carol is the Latin poem *Alleluia! O filii and filiae* (Alleluia, O Sons and Daughters), written by the Franciscan Jean Tisserand (1494) and first published in Paris in 1525. The earliest English translation (Young Men and Maids, Rejoice and Sing) appeared 1748 in a Catholic manual in London. The tune, composed by an unknown musician, was written in Paris, 1623.

Another carol is the German song *Wir wollen alle fröhlich sein* (Let Us All Be Glad), which appeared in a song book (*Christlichs Gesangbüchlein*) in 1568. Geoffry Shaw wrote an English text (Now Glad of Heart Be Every One).

Inspired by Wipo's *Victimae Paschali*, Martin Luther (1546) wrote a dramatic Easter hymn which became a favorite church song among the German Lutherans and later in may other Protestant congregations:

168

It was a strange and wondrous war,
When death and Life did battle.
With royal might did Life prevail,
Made death His knave and chattle.
The sacred Book foretold it all:
How death by death should come to fall.
Now death is laughed to scorn.

In a songbook for students published by the Jesuit Fathers at Cologne in 1695 appeared a Latin Easter hymn (*Finita sunt jam proelia*) that has become a favorite in many countries. An English text was written by Francis Pott in 1861. The modern tune was adapted from Palestrina's *Magnificat Tertii Toni* by William H. Mock in 1861.

The strife is over, the battle done,
The victory of life is won,
The sung of triumph has begun:
      Alleluia.

There are many fine German chorales widely used in Lutheran as well as other Protestant churches. They number several hundred, and among them are some inspiring Easter hymns. The best arrangements of these chorales are found in the works of Johann Sebastian Bach.

Finally, there is a wealth of newer hymns, written in the past few centuries. Charles Wesley (1788)

169

gave us various Easter songs; here are the first and last stanzas of his best-known hymn:

> Christ the Lord is risen today,
> Sons of men, and angels say;
> Raise your joys and triumphs high!
> Sing, ye heavens, and earth reply!
>
> Soar we now where Christ has led,
> Following our exalted Head;
> Made like Him, like Him we rise;
> Ours the cross, the grave, the skies!

Another well-known Easter song is "The World Itself" by John M. Neale (1866). It first appeared in his book *Carols for Eastertide,* in 1854:

> The world itself keeps Easter Day,
>   And Easter larks are singing;
> And Easter flow'rs are blooming gay,
>   And Easter buds are springing.
>   Alleluia, alleluia.
> The Lord of all things lives anew,
> And all His works are living too.
>   Alleluia, alleluia.

The Episcopal Dean Howard Chandler Robbins wrote an "Easter Carol for Children" in 1929 (The Sabbath Day Was By) that has become a popular hymn among Protestant congregations in the United States. Another recent carol is the poem "O Who Shall Roll Away the Stone?" written by Reverend Marion F. Ham, a Unitarian minister. The text was first published in the Boston *Transcript,* in April 1936, and the tune composed by the American organist and choirmaster T. Tertius Noble in 1941.

Of liturgical texts set to music, the best known are the Gradual for Easter, *Haec Dies quam fecit Dominus* (This Is the Day Which the Lord Has Made). This text both in the original Latin or in translations has been set to music by several composers and sung in churches of all Christian denominations. This is also true of the Offertory in the Easter Sunday Mass, *Terra tremuit* (The Earth Trembled).

In Catholic churches the *Regina Coeli Laetare* (Queen of Heaven, Rejoice) is prescribed as antiphon of the Blessed Virgin for Easter time. The text is a fourteenth-century Latin poem, and is sung both in Gregorian chant and various musical settings all through the Easter season. Another hymn often used in Catholic churches is *Regina Coeli Jubila* (Queen of Heaven, Rejoice). This Latin poem appeared first in 1600; the author is unknown.

Among the great oratorios that glorify the Resurrection of Christ, the earliest is Antonio Scandello's

171

Auferstehungsgeschichte (Story of the Resurrection), composed about 1560. It was first performed in the Royal Court Chapel at Dresden.

The latter part of Handel's *Messiah* deals with the Easter story. Every year at its performance thousands are inspired by "I Know that My Redeemer Liveth," and by the "Hallelujah Chorus," during which all audiences traditionally rise from their seats.

Charles Gounod's *Redemption* is another source of familiar Easter music. This work, once very popular, is now rarely performed, though in many churches Easter Day would not be complete without the resounding chorus "Unfold Ye Portals." Similar passages of Easter music are found in the famous choral works of César Franck (*Redemption*) and A. R. Gaul (*The Holy City*).

Of purely instrumental works inspired by the Resurrection, the elaborate overture "Bright Holiday" or "Russian Easter" by Nicholas A. Rimsky-Korsakoff (1908) is most widely known. Based on themes from *Obichod*, a collection of canticles of the Orthodox Church, it presents a vivid picture of the Russian Easter Day celebration.

The "Resurrection Symphony" of Gustav Mahler (1911), while not inspired by the Gospel narrative itself, nevertheless owes it existence to Mahler's con-

172

templation of death and resurrection as a prelude to a new and purified life.

Of the innumerable shorter works, whether choral or instrumental, special mention should be made of Johann Sebastian Bach's several cantatas on Easter texts. There are, of course, also countless short organ pieces inspired by the Resurrection.

Finally, here are a few of the countless popular Easter songs as they exist among all nations.

A Spanish Easter hymn of great power is the song *Jesucristo, Rey Glorioso*, from Ecuador:

> Jesus Christ, the King of glory,
> Lord of goodness, love and light,
> Victor over death and evil,
> Rose in majesty and might.
> Alleluia.
>
> As the Saints in Heaven praise Him
> With their joyful Easter song,
> So on earth, you faithful servants,
> Honor Him with heart and tongue.
> Alleluia.

The Chinese Christians have many beautiful native hymns. An example is the music of an alleluia series, which is attached to the Chinese text of Psalm 112 ("Praise, o servants of the Lord, praise the name of the Lord").[56]

173

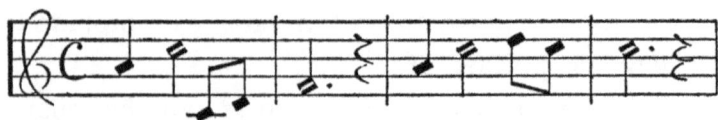

Another example of Chinese music is this traditional alleluia hymn:

Alleluia, alleluia,
O joy to all creation!
Alleluia, alleluia,
The Lord comes forth in glory.

Alleluia, alleluia,
Come, greet the dawn!
Alleluia, alleluia,
The Lord comes forth in glory.

174

An Easter hymn in honor of the glorified body of the Risen Lord is this ancient Tyrolese song (*Ist das der Leib, Herr Jesu Christ*):

Is this thy body, risen Christ,
Which lay in death, all pale and torn?
O Christians come, both young and old,
To see the Lord on Easter morn!
Alleluia, alleluia.

From now through all eternity
This body shines in radiant glow,
More splendid than the noonday-sun:
It will remain forever so.
Alleluia, alleluia.

Thy glory, Christ, I cannot bear,
It is too great for eyes like mine;

175

No one on earth can live and see
The splendor of the Lord divine.
Alleluia, Alleluia.

A free translation of the ancient Latin hymn *Surrexit Christus Hodie* (Christ Is Risen Today) is the Hungarian Easter song *Feltámat Krisztus:*

Christ rose today, alleluia.
All men rejoice, all men rejoice!
Give thanks to the Lord.

Death did He crush, alleluia,
And now He lives, and now He lives.
Give thanks to the Lord.

Love made Him die, alleluia,
And rise again, and rise again.
Give thanks to the Lord.

The Lithuanians sing at Easter the traditional hymn *Linksma diena mums prasvito* (The Joyful Day Has Dawned for Us):

Joyful the day that dawned for us,
The day for which we longed and prayed;
Death died when Christ arose this morn.
Alleluia, alleluia, alleluia.

He broke the reign of death and sin,
Redeemed our souls from Satan's might
And overcame the gates of hell.
Alleluia, alleluia, alleluia.

An angel now in love he sends,
To give the message to his friends:
The Lord is risen, Jesus lives!
Alleluia, alleluia, alleluia.

A jubilant note of Easter joy pervades the music of the traditional Portuguese hymn *A Terra treme* (The Earth Trembled): [57]

An earthquake shook the rocky tomb,
The guards in terror fled.
But Magdalen, in pious haste,
Approaches unafraid.
In love she seeks the Master dear,
Does neither guards nor earthquake fear.
Alleluia, alleluia.

Johann Wolfgang Goethe (1832) indicates in the
Osterlied of his famous poem *Faust*, with classic

brevity and clarity of expression, the basic motif of all popular Easter songs:

> Christ is arisen:
> Joy to all mortals
> Freed from the threatening
> Creeping and deadening
> Serpents of evil.

CHAPTER 15

Easter Symbols and Foods

Among the popular Easter symbols, the lamb is by
far the most significant of this great feast. The Easter
lamb, representing Christ, with the flag of victory,
may be seen in pictures and images in the homes
of every central and eastern European family.

The oldest prayer for the blessing of lambs can be
found in the seventh-century *sacramentary* (ritual
book) of the Benedictine monastery, Bobbio in Italy.
Two hundred years later Rome had adopted it, and
thereafter the main feature of the Pope's Easter dinner for many centuries was roast lamb. After the
tenth century, in place of the whole lamb, smaller

180

pieces of meat were used. In some Benedictine monasteries, however, even today whole lambs are still blessed with the ancient prayers.

The ancient tradition of the Pasch lamb also inspired among the Christians the use of lamb meat as a popular food at Easter time, and at the present time it is eaten as the main meal on Easter Sunday in many parts of eastern Europe. Frequently, however, little figures of a lamb made of butter, pastry, or sugar have been substituted for the meat, forming Easter table centerpieces.

In past centuries it was considered a lucky omen to meet a lamb, especially at Easter time. It was a popular superstition that the devil, who could take the form of all other animals, was never allowed to appear in the shape of a lamb because of its religious symbolism.

The origin of the Easter egg is based on the fertility lore of the Indo-European races. To our pre-Christian ancestors it was a most startling event to see a new and live creature emerge from a seemingly dead object. The egg to them became a symbol of spring. Long ago in Persia people used to present each other with eggs at the spring equinox, which for them also marked the beginning of a new year.[58]

In Christian times the egg had bestowed upon it a religious interpretation, becoming a symbol of the

181

rock tomb out of which Christ emerged to the new life of His Resurrection. There was in addition a very practical reason for making the egg a special sign of Easter joy since it used to be one of the foods that was forbidden in Lent. The faithful from early times painted Easter eggs in gay colors, had them blessed, ate them, and gave them to friends as Easter gifts.

The custom of using Easter eggs developed among the nations of northern Europe and Christian Asia soon after their conversion to Christianity. In countries of southern Europe, and consequently in South America, however, the tradition of Easter eggs never became popular.

The Roman ritual has a special blessing for Easter eggs: [59]

We beseech thee, O Lord, to bestow thy benign blessing upon these eggs, to make them a wholesome food for thy faithful, who gratefully partake of them in honor of the Resurrection of our Lord Jesus Christ.

In medieval times eggs were traditionally given at Easter to all servants. It is reported that King Edward I of England (1307) had 450 eggs boiled before Easter, dyed or covered with gold leaf, which he distributed to the members of the royal household on Easter Day.

The eggs were usually given to children as Easter presents along with other gifts. This practice was so firmly rooted in Germany that the eggs were called *"Dingeier"* (eggs that are "owed"). The children were not slow in demanding what was "owed" to them, and thus developed the many rhymes in France, Germany, Austria, and England, wherein youngsters even today request Easter eggs for presents. In England this custom is called "pace-egging," the word "pace" being a corrupted form of Pasch. Here is a little Austrian song of this kind:

> We sing, we sing the Easter song:
> God keep you healthy, sane and strong.
> Sickness and storms and all other harm
> Be far from folks and beast and farm.
> Now give us eggs, green, blue and red;
> If not, your chicks will all drop dead.

In some parts of Ireland children collect goose and duck eggs during Holy Week, offering them as presents on Easter Sunday. Two weeks previous, on Palm Sunday, they make little nests of stones, and during Holy Week collect as many eggs as possible, storing them away in these hidden nests. On Easter Sunday, they eat them all, sharing with those who are too small to have their own collection.

The grownups, too, give eggs as presents in Ire-

183

land. The number of eggs to be given away is regulated by this ancient saying among Irish country folk: "One egg for the true gentleman; two eggs for the gentleman; three eggs for the churl [have-not]; four eggs for the lowest churl [tramp]."

In most countries the eggs are stained in plain vegetable dye colors. Among the Chaldeans, Syrians, and Greeks, the faithful present each other with crimson eggs in honor of the blood of Christ. In parts of Germany and Austria, green eggs alone are used on Maundy Thursday, but various colors are the vogue at Easter. Some Slavic peoples make special patterns of gold and silver. In Austria artists design striking patterns by fastening ferns and tiny plants around the eggs, which show a white pattern after the eggs are boiled. The Poles and Ukrainians decorate eggs with plain colors or simple designs and call them *krasanki*. Also a number of their eggs are made every year in a most distinctive manner with unusual ornamentation. These eggs are called *pysanki* (from *pysac:* to write, to design); each is a masterpiece of patient labor, native skill, and exquisite workmanship. Melted beeswax is applied with a stylus to the fresh white eggs, which are then dipped in successive baths of dye. After each dipping, wax is painted over the area where the preceding color is to remain. Gradually the whole complex pattern

184

of lines and colors emerges into something fit for a jeweler's window. No two *pysanki* are identical. Although the same symbols are repeated, each egg is designed with great originality. The symbols used most are the sun (good fortune), rooster or hen (fulfillment of wishes), stag or deer (good health), flowers (love and charity). As decorative patterns the artists use rhombic and square checkerboards, dots, wave lines, and intersecting ribbons. The *pysanki* are mainly made by girls and women in painstaking work during the long evenings of Lent. At Easter they are first blessed by the priest and then distributed among relatives, friends, and benefactors. These special eggs are saved from year to year like symbolic heirlooms, and can be seen seasonally in Ukrainian settlements and shops in this country.

In Germany and other countries of central Europe eggs for cooking Easter foods are not broken but pierced with a needle on both ends, and the contents to be used are blown into a bowl. The empty eggshells are given to the children for various Easter games. In parts of Germany such hollow eggs are suspended from shrubs and trees during Easter Week much like a Christmas tree. The Armenians decorate empty eggs with pictures of the Risen Christ, the Blessed Virgin, and other religious designs, to give to children as Easter presents.

185

Easter is the season for games with eggs all over Europe. The sport of egg-pecking is practiced in many forms, in Syria, Iraq, and Iran, as well. In Norway it is called *knekke* (knock). In Germany, Austria, and France, hard-boiled eggs are rolled against each other on the lawn or down a hill; the egg that remains uncracked to the end is called the "victory egg." This game has attained national fame in America through the annual egg-rolling party on the lawn of the White House in Washington.

Here is a description by a visitor to Washington of such a contest several generations ago, when this Easter sport took place on the terraces below the Capitol, and not as in later years on the White House lawn:

At first the children sit sedately in long rows; each has brought a basket of gay-colored, hard-boiled eggs, and those on the upper terraces send them rolling to the line on the next below, and these pass on the ribbon-like-streams to other hundreds at the foot, who scramble for the hopping eggs and hurry panting to the top to start them down again. And, as the sport warms, those on the top who have rolled all the eggs they brought finally roll themselves, shrieking with laughter. Now comes a swirl of curls and ribbons and furbelows, somebody's dainty maid indifferent to bumps and grass-stains. Over yonder

186

a queer eight limbed creature, yelling, gasping, laughing, all at once shakes itself apart into two slender boys racing toward the top to come down again. Another set of boys who started in a line of six with joined hands are trying to come down in somersaults without breaking the chain. On all sides the older folk stand by to watch the games of this infant Carnival which comes to an end only when the children are forced away by fatigue to the point of exhaustion, or by parental order. No one seems to know how the custom began.

The observation is also made that "when the games proved too hard a test for the grass on the Capitol terraces, Congress stopped the practice, and the President opened the slope back of the White House." [60] In recent years, it might be added, the grass there has received the same sort of treatment as the Capitol terraces a few generations ago. The custom of egg-rolling in Washington is traced back to Sunday School picnics and parades at Easter in the years before the Civil War. At these picnics the children amused themselves with various games, and egg-rolling was one of them.

Another universal custom among children is the egg hunting in house and garden on Easter Sunday morning. In France children are told that the Easter eggs are dropped by the church bells on their return

187

from Rome. In Germany and Austria little nests containing eggs, pastry, and candy are placed in hidden spots, and the children believe that the Easter bunny so popular in this country, too, has laid the eggs and brought the candy.

In Russia and among the Ukrainians and Poles people start their joyful Easter meals after the long Lenten fast with a blessed egg on Easter Sunday. Before sitting down to breakfast, the father solemnly distributes small pieces cut from an Easter egg to members of the family and guests, wishing them one and all a holy and happy feast. Not until they have eaten this morsel in silence, do they sit down to the first meal of the Easter season.

The Easter bunny had its origin in pre-Christian fertility lore. Hare and rabbit were the most fertile animals our forefathers knew, serving as symbols of abundant new life in the spring season. The Easter bunny has never had a religious symbolism bestowed on its festive usage, though its white meat is sometimes said to suggest purity and innocence. The Church has never performed special blessings for rabbits or hares, and neither in the liturgy nor in folklore do we find these animals linked with the spiritual meanings of the sacred season. However, the bunny has acquired a cherished role in the celebration of Easter as the legendary producer of Easter eggs for children in many countries.

What seems to be the first mention of the Easter bunny and his eggs is a short admonition in a German book of 1572: "Do not worry if the bunny escapes you; should we miss his eggs, then we shall cook the nest." In a German book of the seventeenth century the story that the Easter bunny lays eggs and hides them in the garden, is called "an old fable." [61]

In many sections of Germany the Easter bunny was believed to lay red eggs on Maundy Thursday and eggs of other colors the night before Easter Sunday. The first Easter bunnies made of pastry and sugar were popular in southern Germany at the beginning of the last century. They are now a favorite delicacy for children in many lands.

Let us not forget the pig, which offers its meat as a traditional Easter dish. This animal has always been a symbol of good luck and prosperity among the Indo-Europeans. Many traces of this ancient symbolism are still alive in our time. In some German popular expressions the word "pig" is synonymous with "good luck" (*Schwein haben*). In Hungary the highest card (ace) in card games is called "pig" (*diszn*ó). Not too long ago it was fashionable for men to wear little figures of pigs as good luck charms on their watch chains. More recently charm bracelets for teen-agers contained dangling pigs. Savings boxes for children in the figure of a pig (piggy banks) carry out the ancient symbolism of good luck and prosperity.

It is an age-old custom, handed down from pre-Christian times, to eat the meat of this animal on festive occasions. Thus the English and Scandinavians ate boar meat and the Germans and Slavs roast pork on Christmas Day. Also, in many parts of Europe roast pork is still the traditional main dish at weddings and on major feast days. At Easter, smoked or cooked ham, as well as lamb, has been eaten by most European nations from ancient times, and is the traditional Easter dish from coast to coast in this country. Roast pork is another traditional main dish in some countries.

The nations of central and eastern Europe have other traditional Easter foods, prepared on the last days of Holy Week, blessed by the priest on Holy Saturday or Easter Sunday, and solemnly displayed on a festive table for Easter Week meals. This blessed Easter fare is called *Weihessen* (blessed food) in Germany and Austria, *Swiecone* or *Swieconka* (sanctified) among the Ukrainians and Poles. The figure of the Easter lamb, which rests on a bedding of evergreen twigs, is surrounded by colored

190

Easter eggs. Around this centerpiece are arranged other foods in great variety and large amounts: Easter breads, meats, sausages, salads, cheese, pastry, spices, and fruit. The whole table and every dish on it are decorated with garlands and clusters of leaves, herbs, and flowers. It would be impossible to include in one small book the traditional Easter fare of every nationality. Here are a few of the better-known dishes:

The Russian Easter bread (*paska*) is made of flour, cottage cheese, sugar, raisins, eggs, and milk. It is put in a mold and shaped in firm, square pieces, about eight inches high, with a cross on each side, and the letters J. C. (Jesus Christ) imprinted in relief. In Germany and Austria the Easter bread is made with milk, eggs, and raisins, and baked in oblong loaves of twisted or braided strands (*Osterstollen*). Another kind of Austrian Easter bread is the *Osterlaib* (Easter loaf), a large, flat round loaf marked with the cross or an image of the lamb. In some parts of Ireland people eat on Easter Sunday "Golden bread" which is very similar to our French toast.

A favorite Easter pastry in Poland are the *mazurki*, originating in the province of Mazuria, which are very sweet cakes made with honey and filled with nuts and fruit. The most popular of the coffee cakes

191

in Poland and other countries, too, is called *baba,* a provincialism for woman. The cake is always baked in a fluted pan. It resembles the skirt of a woman. *Babka,* a word commonly used for grandmother, is the same cake but in a smaller size. *Babecska* is the diminution of the word. Small rolls or cupcakes are called *babeczki.* Here is a good recipe for Easter *baba* (*Baba Wielkanocna*):

1 cup milk	1 tsp. vanilla
3 cups flour	¼ tsp. almond flavoring
¼ cup lukewarm milk	1 cup chopped almonds
2 yeast cakes	1 cup chopped citron,
½ cup plus 1 tbsp. sugar	orange and lemon peel
2 tsp. salt	½ cup melted butter
15 egg yolks	bread crumbs

Scald the milk. Slowly add three-quarters cup flour to hot milk and beat thoroughly. Cool. Dissolve yeast in quarter cup of milk and a tablespoon of sugar and add to cooled mixture. Beat well. Let rise until double in bulk. Add salt to eggs and beat until thick and lemon-colored. Add sugar and continue to beat. Add to sponge with flavoring and remaining flour. Knead for ten minutes. Add butter and continue kneading for ten more minutes or until dough leaves the fingers. Add almonds and citron peels and mix well. Let rise until double in bulk. Punch down and let rise again. Punch down and put into fluted tube pan. Butter the pan, press blanched almonds around the sides and bottom. Sprinkle with fine bread crumbs. Fill with dough to cover one-third of the pan and let rise one hour. Bake 50 minutes at 350°. Sprinkle with colored sugar or baker's confetti.

Another delightful Easter delicacy are the Papal Wafers, called *Sucharki Papieskie:*

⅔ cup butter	1 whole egg
7 egg yolks	2 cups flour
½ cup sugar	1 tsp. baking soda

Cream butter, add alternately one egg yolk and one tablespoon sugar and beat well. Add the whole egg. Add flour and oaking soda. Mix well. Put on floured board, roll to ¼ inch thickness and cut with round cookie cutter. Bake on well buttered baking sheet in 375° oven for 12 to 15 minutes.[62]

An Austrian pastry is the *Weihkuchen* (blessed cake) made of flour, oil, milk, butter, and honey. The people of Transylvania bake their ham in a cover of bread dough. The Hungarian Easter meat loaf is made of chopped pork, ham, eggs, bread, and spices.

About thirty years ago breweries in Norway started to make a special Easter beer (*Paskelbrygg*), a blend of the best beers made locally. It became very popular, and today *Paskelbrygg* is a favorite addition to traditional Easter fare in Scandinavia.

193

CHAPTER 16

The Easter Season

In the early days of Christianity all of Easter Week was one continuous feast. Although the number of prescribed holydays differed in various provinces, most people abstained from their usual work and attended church services every day. Many went to all three services that at the time of the Roman Empire were held daily at morning, noon, and night. Priests in France used to celebrate two Masses every day during Easter Week. Indeed, a Spanish Missal of the ninth century shows three Mass texts for each day of the Easter Octave.

Gradually, however, the Church reduced obligatory attendance to four days, then, in 1094, to three. In many parts of Europe these three days are still observed, at least as half holydays, which means that most of the faithful, although not obliged to attend Mass, voluntarily do so, as well as abstain from work. Since 1911, even Easter Monday is no longer a holyday of obligation though it remains a legal holiday in most European countries, both Catholic and Protestant.

Because those who were baptized on Holy Saturday wore new white garments, Easter Week is also called "White Week" in the Western Church and the "Week of New Garments" in the Oriental Church. During the whole week the newly baptized, in their linen dress and soft sandals, stood close to the altar at all services as a separate group within the sanctuary of the basilica. Every day the bishop would address them with special instructions after the other worshipers had left. It was the honeymoon of their new life as Christians, a week of intense happiness and spiritual joy. On the Sunday after Easter they attended Mass clothed for the last time in their white baptismal robes. At the end of the service the bishop solemnly dismissed them from the place of honor in the sanctuary, so they could mix with their families and friends in the body of the church. Later, at home, they would exchange the white garments for

195

the ordinary dress of their station in life. The significance of this change is still preserved in the official
name of Low Sunday, "Sunday in White" (*Dominica
in Albis*), meaning the last day on which the white
garments are worn.

Easter Monday was, in medieval times, and still
is in many countries, a day of rest, relaxation, and
special festivities. First among them is the "Emmaus
walk," a custom inspired by the Gospel of the day
(Luke 24, 13-35). Families and groups of friends go
on outings or long walks into the fields, forests, and
mountains, hold picnics and spend the afternoon
playing games, dancing, and singing. In Germany
and Austria long ago, youngsters would gather in
large meadows to play Easter games and Easter
sports (*Osterspiele*), and also to perform ancient
folk dances accompanied by the music of guitars
and mandolins. The piece of land on which these
Easter games took place bore the name "Easter field"
(*Osteranger*), and many cities still have lots so
called, although the custom has long since vanished.
In the rural regions, however, such ancient traditions
have survived and are practiced every year.

In French Canada the Emmaus walk takes the
form of a visit to the grandparents, which is faithfully adhered to by all children on Easter Monday.
The Poles hold their outings and picnics in large

groups, often the inhabitants of a whole town will gather in some rural "Emmaus" grove which remains the goal of their excursions for many years. The days from Holy Thursday to Easter Tuesday are observed as public holidays in Norway, and many people spend this period in skiing and other winter sports in the snowy hills. In the *Nordmarke* (a skiing territory outside the city of Oslo) a Lutheran chapel has been erected where Easter services are held for holiday guests at the camps. The deep tan acquired in the open air during the Easter holidays is called *Paskebrun* (Easter tan).

In most countries of northern Europe, Monday and Tuesday are the traditional days of "switching" and "drenching," customs based on pre-Christian fertility rites, previously mentioned. On Monday the boys are supposed to apply this ancient rite to the girls, while on Tuesday the girls retaliate. Actually both are now performed on Easter Monday in many places. The custom is called *Gsundschlagen* (stroke of health) in Austria and southern Germany, *Dyngus* (ransom) in Poland, *Loscolkodas* (dousing) in Hungary, and *Pomlazka* (willow switch) among the Czechs and Slovaks. In good-natured mischief the boys will surprise the girls with buckets or bottles of water, and douse them thoroughly, often reciting some little rhyme like this:

197

Water for your health,
Water for your home,
Water for your land:
  Here's water, water!
  It's better than sand.
Don't shriek and cry and run away;
It's good for you on Dyngus day.

Whole processions are formed by youngsters dressed in outlandish costumes who go from farm to farm and sing or recite playful ditties. At the end of their performance they suddenly splash water on their host and his family, whereupon they are given eggs, pastry, and sweets. In many places the water is merely sprinkled instead of splashed, and in cities people have refined the ancient custom by spraying perfume at each other with friendly wishes for good health and happiness.

The "switching" is done with gentleness. Carrying their rods of pussy willow or leaved branches, the boys go in little groups from house to house, apply the switch to all women (but never to children), and receive small presents in reward. Groups of girls carry a little tree or branch, decorated with flowers and ribbons. They make the rounds like the boys, and at every home they sing traditional songs announcing the summer and expressing good wishes for health and harvest. On Quinquagesima Sunday in Norway young folks visit relatives and friends and "spank" them with the *Fastelavns-ris* (carnival rod), which is made of brightly colored paper strips fastened to a painted stick or handle.

A custom of considerable antiquity was that of "heaving," practiced in England in the counties of Shropshire, Cheshire, and Lancashire on Easter Monday and Tuesday up through the nineteenth century. Some small villages may still do it. On Easter Monday a group of men go to each house carrying a chair aloft, and amid much excitement and joking insist that any lady present get into the chair and be lifted up three times as they shout huzzas, demanding a forfeit in the form of a kiss. On the next day it is the girls' turn to do the same thing to the men. Could the expression and action of giving someone the "old heave-ho" have come from this quaint Easter custom? This is the way it appeared to a startled gentleman in Shrewsbury who, in 1799, wrote:

I was sitting alone last Easter Tuesday at breakfast at the Talbot at Shrewsbury, when I was surprised by the entrance of all the female servants of the house handing in an arm-chair of different colors. I asked them what they wanted. Their answer was, they came to *heave* me. It was the custom of the place on that morning, and they hoped I would take a seat in their chair. It was impossible

199

not to comply with a request very modestly made, and to a set of young nymphs in their best apparel. I wished to see all the ceremony, and seated myself accordingly. The group lifted me from the ground, turned the chair about, and I had the felicity of a salute from each. I told them I supposed there was a fee due upon the occasion, and was answered in the affirmative; and having satisfied the damsels in this respect, they withdrew to *heave* others. On inquiry I found that on Easter Monday between nine and twelve, the men heave the women in the same manner.

Among Slavic nations the Thursday of Easter Week is devoted in a special way to the "Easter memory" of the departed ones. The faithful go to Mass, which on this particular day is offered for the dead of the parish. Pictures of deceased relatives and friends are decorated with flowers both at home and in the cemetery (many tombstones carry images of the deceased, usually a framed photograph). No farmer would work on this day, for the memory of the holy souls demands respectful rest and quiet. According to popular superstition any man who works his farm on Easter Thursday will meet with ill luck and dire punishment.

Friday of Easter Week is a favorite day for devout pilgrimages (*Osterwallfahrt*) in many parts of Europe. Praying and singing hymns the faithful walk many hours through fields and forests, preceded by a cross and many church banners. The goal of the pilgrimage is usually a shrine or church in some other neighborhood village. There they attend Mass and perform their devotions. At one of these processions, in the Austrian Tyrol, people walk ten hours each way. In some sections of Germany and Austria the farmers make their pilgrimage on horseback, accompanied by a band playing Easter hymns.

The Sunday after Easter (White Sunday) is called "Low Sunday" in English-speaking countries, so named because Easter actually lasts eight days including two Sundays—the primary (high) one is Easter Sunday, and the secondary (low) the Sunday after Easter.

Low Sunday was for centuries, and still is in most parts of Europe, the day when the children receive their First Communion. Dressed in white, they enter the church in solemn procession, holding lighted candles. They renew their baptismal vows and assist at Mass, which usually is conducted with great solemnity. In some places a most appealing custom is observed. Each child receives the Blessed Sacrament with father and mother kneeling beside him. People in Europe traditionally call this event the "most beautiful day of life."

On Thursday of the sixth week after Easter (forty

201

days after Easter Sunday) the Church celebrates the Feast of the Ascension. According to the Bible, on that day the Lord commissioned His apostles to preach the Gospel to all nations; then, having blessed them, He "was lifted up before their eyes, and a cloud took him out of their sight" (Acts 1, 9).

The feast that commemorates this event is of very ancient origin. The first mention of it is found in the writings of Eusebius, Bishop of Nicomedia (341).[63] At the end of the fourth century it was universally celebrated in the whole Roman Empire. Saint Augustine attributes its origin to the apostles themselves.

In those early centuries a procession took place in Rome on Ascension Day around noontime, in memory of the apostles accompanying Christ to the Mount at Olivet. The Pope with the assisting clergy walked from the Lateran to a church or shrine outside the walls, where the Gospel of the Ascension was read and a prayer service held. This custom was soon introduced as a universal rite in the whole Western Church. In later centuries some dramatic details were added, as in Germany where two priests would lift a cross aloft when the words *Ascendo ad Patrem* (I go up to the Father) were sung. From the eleventh to the fourteenth centuries, such symbolic actions gradually developed into dramas and church

202

plays. It became a cherished custom in many European countries to enact the Ascension by hoisting a statue of the Risen Christ aloft until it disappeared through an opening in the ceiling of the church. While the image, suspended on a rope, moved slowly upward, the people rose in their pews and stretched out their arms toward the figure of the Savior, acclaiming the Lord in prayer or by hymn singing. Hundreds of reports in old books from the fourteenth to the seventeenth centuries contain vivid descriptions of this ancient custom.

One of the most charming examples is the Ascension Play of the Bavarian monastery in Moosburg, recorded by the priest and poet Johann von Berghausen (1362). [64] In the center of the church, directly underneath an opening in the ceiling, a platform decorated with colored cloths and flowers was erected. On this platform stood a little tent, open on the top, which represented the Mount of Olivet. Inside the tent was placed a statue of the Risen Christ, holding high the banner of victory. A strong rope that hung down from the ceiling was fastened to a ring on top of the wooden image. After Vespers (in the afternoon), a solemn procession moved from the sacristy to the platform. It was led by two boys in white dresses. They impersonated angels; on the shoulders they wore wings and on their heads little

203

wreaths of flowers. They were followed by a young cleric who represented the Blessed Virgin, "dressed in the robes of holy and honorable widowhood." To his right and left walked clerics enacting Saint Peter and Saint John. Behind them came ten other clerics in oriental gowns; they were barefoot, and on their foreheads they carried diadems inscribed with the names of the apostles. The altar boys and priests, vested in festive garb, concluded the group. In front of the platform, the deacon sang the Gospel of Ascension Day, and the choir intoned the antiphon, "I ascend to my Father and your Father, to my God and your God" (John 20, 17). The priests then venerated the image of Christ with inclinations and incense. Finally, while the choir sang, *Ascendit Deus in altum, alleluia* (God rose on high), the statue was slowly pulled aloft. As it rose higher and higher, a few figures of angels holding burning candles came down from "Heaven" to meet the Lord and to accompany him on his journey. From a large metal ring that was suspended below the opening, there hung cloths of silk representing clouds. Between these "clouds" the image of the Savior slowly and solemnly disappeared. A few moments later, a shower of roses, lilies, and other flowers dropped from the opening; then followed wafers in the shape of large hosts. The school children were allowed to collect these flowers and wafers, to take them home as cherished souvenirs. Father Berghausen explains this custom as follows: "The little ones collect the flowers which symbolize the various gifts of the Holy Spirit. The wafers indicate the presence of Christ in His eucharistic Body, which remains with us, under the species of bread, to the end of time." While the congregation stood with eyes raised to the ceiling, the two "angels" intoned the final message of Ascension Day, which predicts the triumphant coming of the Lord on the clouds of Heaven, for the great judgment at the end of the world: "Why do you stand looking up to heaven? This Jesus, who has been taken up from you into heaven, shall come in the same way as you have seen him going up to heaven" (Acts 1, 11). The celebration was concluded with solemn Benediction.

In many towns of the Austrian Tyrol such plays were performed up to the present century. Sometimes it would happen that one of the angel figures which met the statue of Christ in mid-air had its candle blown out by a draft; in such cases the angel would quickly fly back to "heaven" to have it lit again, and with brightly burning light would slowly return, to the great glee and enjoyment of all the children in church.

The Lutheran Reformers raised a great hue and

cry not only against some abuses in these plays but against the whole institution, calling it an outrage and blasphemy. However, Luther himself seems to have later regretted the hasty condemnations of earlier years, for in a message to his preachers he wrote, in 1530: "If such customs had remained as pageants for the sake of youth and school children, to furnish them with a presentation of Christian doctrine and Christian life, then it could well be allowed that Palm donkeys, Ascension plays, and many similar traditions might be admitted and tolerated; for by such things conscience is not led into confusion." [65]

It was a widespread custom in many parts of Europe during the Middle Ages to eat a bird on Ascension Day, because Christ "flew" to Heaven. Pigeons, pheasants, partridges, and even crows, graced the dinner tables. In Western Germany bakers and innkeepers gave their customers pieces of pastry made in the shapes of various birds. In England the feast was celebrated with games, dancing, and horse races. In central Europe, Ascension Day is a traditional day of mountain climbing and picnics on hill tops and high places.

A simple but impressive liturgical ceremony has survived to our day. After the Gospel of the Mass, in which the event of Christ's Ascension is related, the Easter candle is extinguished in every Catholic church. Through forty days it had stood next to the main altar, its low flame symbolizing the Risen Life of the Savior. Now that the Lord has returned to Heaven, the symbolic light of his visible presence on earth is extinguished.

Although the Church includes the Feast of Pentecost (the day the Holy Ghost descended on the apostles) in the liturgical season of Easter, it is actually Ascension Day that terminates the events of the Savior's life on earth. Henceforth all followers of Christ "look up to Heaven" (Acts 1, 11) where He "sits at the right hand of God" (Mark 16, 19), and whence He shall come to judge the living and the dead. An unknown poet of the Middle English period wrote, at the end of his poem on the Passion of Christ, a short prayer that comprehends the meaning both of Ascension Day and of the whole Easter season in these few touching words:

> Jesus,
> As to the skies
> Thou did'st arise,
> Raise us!
> Amen.[66]

Lenten and Easter Calendar

The following calendar of Lenten and Easter days as they are used in Catholic and many Protestant churches may be helpful as a point of reference throughout this book. The Gospel of the day and pertinent passages from the Bible are indicated wherever the liturgical service commemorates certain events of the life of Christ.

PRE-LENT

Septuagesima Sunday. The Alleluia is discontinued in all
services of the liturgy.
 Sunday Gospel: Matthew 20, 1-16.

Sexagesima Sunday. On Thursday after Sexagesima begins the Carnival season.

Sunday Gospel: Luke 8, 4-15.

Quinquagesima Sunday (Carnival Sunday). Tuesday (Shrove Tuesday, Mardi Gras) ends the Carnival season.

Sunday Gospel: Luke 18, 31-43.

LENT

Ash Wednesday. Imposition of blessed ashes; beginning of the forty days' fast.

Bible: The fast and temptation of Christ (Matthew 4, 1-11; Mark 1, 12; Luke 4, 1-12).

First Sunday of Lent. (*Invocabit* Sunday, from the first word of the Latin Mass text).

Sunday Gospel: Matthew 4, 1-11.

Second Sunday of Lent (*Reminiscere*).

Sunday Gospel: Matthew 17, 1-9.

Third Sunday of Lent (*Oculi*).

Sunday Gospel: Luke 11, 14-28.

Fourth Sunday of Lent (*Laetare;* Mid-Lent Sunday)

Sunday Gospel: John 6, 1-15.

Passion Sunday (*Judica*). Beginning of Passiontide. On Friday after Passion Sunday is the Feast of the Seven Sorrows of the Blessed Virgin Mary.

Sunday Gospel: John 8, 46-59.

HOLY WEEK

Palm Sunday (Hosanna Sunday). Blessing and distribution of palms. During Mass, chanting of St. Matthew's Passion (Matthew 26, 1–27, 66).

Sunday Gospel: Matthew 21, 1-9.

Monday in Holy Week. Gospel: John 12, 1-9.

Tuesday in Holy Week. During Mass, reading of St. Mark's Passion (Mark 14, 1–15, 46).

Wednesday in Holy Week. During Mass, reading of St. Luke's Passion (Luke 22, 1–23, 53). In the afternoon or evening, the *Tenebrae* are held.

Maundy Thursday (Holy Thursday). After Mass, procession to Repository shrine. Stripping of altars. Ceremony of the washing of feet. *Tenebrae* in the afternoon or evening.

Bible: Last Supper—Matthew 26, 3-35
           Mark 14, 1-31
           Luke 22, 1-33
           John 13, 1–17, 26

    Agony and Arrest of Christ—Matthew 26, 36-56
                    Mark 14, 32-43
                    Luke 22, 39-53
                    John 18, 1-12

    Other Events of Thursday night—
                    Matthew 26, 57-75
                    Mark 14, 53-72
                    Luke 22, 54-65
                    John 18, 13-27

Good Friday. Chanting of St. John's Passion (John 18, 1–19, 42). Prayer service. Adoration of the Cross. Mass of the Presanctified. *Tenebrae* in the afternoon.

Extra-liturgical Observances: Shrine of the Sepulcher; Three Hours' devotion; Oratorios on the Passion; Processions and Passion plays.

Bible: Trials and condemnation of Christ—

> Matthew 27, 1-31
> Mark 15, 1-20
> Luke 22, 66–23, 24
> John 18, 28–19, 16

Crucifixion and death of Christ—

> Matthew 27, 32-56
> Mark 15, 21-41
> Luke 23, 25-49
> John 19, 17-37

Burial of Christ—Matthew 27, 57-61

> Mark 15, 42-47
> Luke 23, 50-56
> John 19, 38-42

Holy Saturday. End of Lenten fast (at noon). No liturgical service provided for the day. However, the night vigil of Easter Sunday has been advanced to Saturday morning for centuries.

Easter Vigil Service (usually held on Saturday morning): Blessing of Fire and procession of lights; *Exultet* (Easter song) and lighting of Easter candle; Blessing of Baptismal water; Litanies; Mass. At this Vigil service the Alleluia is resumed.

211

Extra-liturgical Observances: Shrine of the Sepulcher;
Resurrection service in the evening.

Bible: Sabbath rest of disciples: Luke 23, 56
Roman guard at the tomb: Matthew 27, 62-66

EASTER

Easter Sunday. Feast of the Resurrection. Greatest liturgical feast day of the year.

Bible: The Resurrection—Matthew 28, 2-7
Mark 16, 1-7
Luke 24, 1-12
John 20, 1-13
Apparitions of Christ—Matthew 28, 8-10
Mark 16, 9-13
Luke 24, 13-43
John 20, 14-23
The Guards and the Chief Priests—
Matthew 28, 11-15.

Easter Monday (Emmaus Day).
Gospel of the day: Luke 24, 13-35.
Low Sunday (White Sunday), first Sunday after Easter.
Sunday Gospel: John 20, 19-31.
Second Sunday after Easter.
Sunday Gospel: John 10, 11-16.
Third Sunday after Easter.
Sunday Gospel: John 16, 16-22.
Fourth Sunday after Easter.
Sunday Gospel: John 16, 5-14.

Fifth Sunday after Easter.

  Sunday Gospel: John 16, 23-30.

  Bible: The Apparitions of Christ between Easter Sunday and Ascension Day—Matthew 28, 16-20

Mark 16, 12-13

Luke 24, 34-43

John 20, 19–21, 24

Ascension Day (Thursday of the fifth Week after Easter).

  Bible: Matthew 16, 14-20 (Gospel of the Day)

Luke 24, 44-53

Acts 1, 1-11.

Dates for Ash Wednesday and Easter

1954	March 3	April 18
1955	February 23	April 10
1956	February 15	April 1
1957	March 6	April 21
1958	February 19	April 6
1959	February 11	March 29
1960	March 2	April 17
1961	February 15	April 2
1962	March 7	April 22
1963	February 27	April 14
1964	February 12	March 29
1965	March 3	April 18

213

Reference Notes

1. These "fertility cults" are *not* the Greek cults of the same name, but a part of the general practice of nature lore among the Indo-Europeans. On the background of ancient spring lore, see Eugen Mogk, *Germanische Religionsgeschichte und Mythologie*, Berlin, 1921; Hanns Koren, *Volksbrauch im Kirchenjahr*, Leipzig, 1934; G. Graber, *Der Schlag mit der Lebensrute*, Klagenfurt, 1910; Adolf Spamer, *Deutsche Fastnachtsbräuche*, Jena, 1936.
2. A German version is in Victor Geramb, *Sitte und Brauch in Oesterreich*, Graz, 1948, p. 47.
3. Daniel J. Foley, "Mary Gardens," in *The Herbarist*, Boston, 1953, No. 19.
4. Official liturgical prayer of the Church recited daily by clerics in major orders and also by many religious both male and female.
5. *De Ecclesiasticis Officiis*, I, 13; J. P. Migne, PL (*Patrologia Latina*), vol. LXXXIII, col. 750.
6. *Liber de Oratione*, chap. 27; PL, vol. I, col. 1194.
7. *Ad Marcellam Epistola*, p. 46; PL, vol. XXII, col. 491.
8. *De Cantico Novo*, chap. 2; PL, vol. XL, col. 680.
9. *Epistolarum Liber II*, ep. 10; PL, vol. LVIII, col. 488.
10. *Historia Gentis Anglorum*, lib. I, chap. 20; PL, vol. XCV, col. 49.
11. St. Jerome, *De Morte Fabiolae*, ep. 77; PL, vol. XXII, chap. 697. Also *Acta Sanctorum* (Boland.), August 3, p. 83 (on the burial service of St. Radegundis).

12. Gulielmus Durandus (senior), *Rationale Divinorum Officiorum*, lib. VI, chap. 24, par. 18.

13. *The Hymnal of the Protestant Episcopal Church in the United States of America 1940*, New York, 1943, Hymn No. 54.

14. Karl Young, *The Drama of the Medieval Church*, Oxford, 1933, vol. I, p. 552 (Latin text).

15. Clemens Blume, *Des Alleluja Leben, Begräbnis und Auferstehung*, in *Stimmen aus Maria Laach*, Freiburg, 1897, vol. I, p. 429 (Latin text).

16. Quoted in Herbert Thurston, *Lent and Holy Week*, London, 1904, p. 62.

17. The New York *Times*, February 19, 1953.

18. *De Penitentia*, chap. XI; PL, vol. I, col. 1246.

19. Psalms No. 6, 31, 37, 50, 101, 129, 142.

20. MS 400.265, Oxford University. See *English Historical Review*, 1895, p. 727 ff.

21. A. G. *Busbequii Legationis Turcicae Epistolae IV*, Paris, 1589.

22. Encyclical *Inter Cetera*, of January 1, 1748.

23. F. Van der Meer, *Augustinus als Seelsorger*, Köln, 1951, p. 429 ff.

24. *Letters* of St. Athanasius (translated and quoted by St. Jerome); PL, vol. XXII, col. 773 ff.

25. Correct dates for Ash Wednesday and Easter Sunday from 1954 to 1965 are on page 213.

26. *Epistolae;* PL, vol. LXXVII, col. 1352.

27. J. P. Migne, PG (*Patrologia Graeca*), vol. XXXI, col. 186.

28. *Gen. Homiliae X*, chap. I; PG, vol. LIII, col. 82.

29. "*Sit abstinentia jejunantis refectio pauperis,*" Sermo XIII; PL, vol. LIV, col. 172.

30. Codex No. 3867, Vatican Library.

31. *Homilia;* PL, vol. CCXVII, col. 393.

32. *The Oxford Book of Carols,* edited by P. Dearmer, R. V. Williams, M. Shaw, London, 1941, p. 292.

33. Hymn No. 61.

34. Nicolaus Nilles, S.J., *Kalendarium Manuale untriusque Ecclesiae,* Innsbruck, 1897, vol. II, p. 212 ff.

35. Lanfrancus, *Ordinationes,* sect. 4; PL, vol. CL, col. 455.

36. *Ceremoniale Episcoporum,* lib. II, chap. XXI, rub. 2.

37. *Missale Romanum, Dominica in Palmis (Benedictio Ramorum).*

38. *"Fit fragor et strepitus aliquantulum,"* rubric after the Lauds of Holy Thursday, in the Roman breviary.

39. Roman Breviary, Responsory, third nocturne of the Matins of Good Friday.

40. *Epistolae,* vol. 54, chap. VII, p. 10 (Edit. Maur.).

41. *Epistola;* PL, vol. III, col. 12.

42. From *Lyra Liturgica.*

43. See Young, *Drama of the Medieval Church,* vol. I, p. 112 ff.

44. *The Devotion of the Three Hours of Agony,* anon., London, 1806.

45. *The Cambridge History of English Literature,* New York, 1907, vol. I, p. 301 ff.

46. St. Augustine, *Sermo* CCXIX; PL, vol. XXXVIII, col. 1088. The other expressions are taken from the *Exultet* (Liturgy of Holy Saturday).

47. Eusebius, *De Vita Constantini,* lib. IV, chap. 22; PL, vol. VIII, col. 75.

48. *Oratio IV in s. Pascha;* PG, vol. XLVI, col. 681.

49. Louis Gougaud, O.S.B., *Christianity in Celtic Lands,* London, 1932, p. 279 ff.

50. *Oratio in Paschate,* p. 42; PG, vol. XLVI, col. 683.

51. *De Temporum Ratione,* chap. 15; PL, vol. XC, col. 357.

52. Fynes Morrison, *Itinerary;* see Thurston, *Lent and Holy Week,* p. 237.

53. A German text in Josef Pommer, *Das Deutsche Volkslied,* Wien, 1905, p. 63.

54. Johannes Pauli, *Schimpf und Ernst,* Vienna, 1522; J. J. Zeller, *Das beschämte Laster,* Augsburg, 1771.

55. *The Hymnal of the Protestant Episcopal Church* . . . , Hymns No. 93, 94, 95.

56. Chang Wen Yeh, *Collection of Religious Hymns,* Peiping, 1947, vol. I, p. 8.

57. Musical setting by M. F. McCarthy, S.J., and R. E. Maloney, S.J.

58. Albert Becker, *Osterei und Osterhase,* Jena, 1937; H. Hepding, *Ostereier und Osterhase,* in *Hessische Berichte für Volkskunde,* vol. XXVI, 1927.

59. *Rituale Romanum, Benedictio ovorum.*

60. *The Book of Easter,* edited by G. W. Edwards, p. 93.

61. *De ovibus paschalibus. Von Oster-Eyern, Satyrae medicae,* 1682. See Gustav Gugitz, *Das Jahr und seine Feste,* Wien, 1949, vol. I, p. 188.

62. From *Treasured Polish Recipes for Americans,* Polanie Publishing Co., Minneapolis, 1948, pp. 124-146.

63. *De solemnitate Paschae,* chap. V; PL, vol. XXIV, col. 699.

64. Neil C. Brooks, *Das Moosburger Himmelfahrtspiel,* in *Zeitschrift für deutsches Altertum,* 1925, vol. LX, p. 91.

65. Martin Luther, *Vermahnung an die Geistlichen zu Augsburg,* 1530.

66. E. Morris, *A Song of the Passion,* Early English Text Society, London, 1872, vol. XLIX.

Index

Abelard, Peter, 86
Abstinence, 35-6; *see also* Fasting, Pre-Lent
Adoration of the Cross, 114, 115
Advent, 13
Agde, Council of, 152
Agnus Dei, 140
Alabama, 40
Alexander II, Pope, 27, 29
Alexandria, Egypt, 56, 57; Archbishop of, 57
Allegri, Gregorio, 100
Alleluia, 27-33, 154; Burial of, 31-2
Almond Day, 110
Ambrose, St., 165, 166
Ambrosius, St., 112
America, 93
Angelus, 148
Annunciation, Feast of the, 20
Apostolic Constitutions, 112
Apollinaris, Sidonius, 28
Armenia, 94, 185
Ascension Day, 202, 204-7
Ascension, Feast of the, 202
Ash Wednesday, 35-7, 40, 43-6, 48-50, 53, 58, 66, 69, 107, 152; other names for, 35, 37
Ashes, 43-6, 48-51, 54
Asia Minor, 59
Athanasius, St., 56
Augustine, St., 28, 53, 100, 104, 165, 202
Augustine of Canterbury, St., 58
Austria, 16, 18, 23, 26, 38, 50, 66, 74, 75, 96, 100, 102, 111,

128, 144, 158, 160, 161, 183, 184, 186, 188, 190, 191, 193, 196, 197, 201
Auxerre, France, Church of, 30
Azores, 110

Bach, J. S., 76, 87, 124, 169, 173
Bach Choir, 124
Bangor, Maine, 87
Baptism, 52, 53, 132-3, 136, 148, 195
Basil the Great, St., 59
Bavaria, 51, 89, 96
Bede the Venerable, St., 29, 149
Beer, 193
Beethoven, Ludwig van, 124
Bells, 50, 92, 105-6, 110, 111, 142, 153, 154, 158, 162, 187
Benedict XIII, Pope, 81
Benedict XIV, Pope, 42, 49-50
Benedictine order, 60; monasteries, 180, 181
Benedictis, Jacobus de, *see* Todi, Jacopone da
Berghausen, Johann von, 203, 205
Bethlehem, 139
Bethlehem, Pennsylvania, 124, 159
Bitter Sorrows, 77-8
"Black fast," 126
Blau, Eduard, 125
Bobbio, Abbey of, 90, 180
Bohemia, 75
Bouquet, bridal, 25
Bread, 143, 191